# It Was No Accident

One Family's Life Interrupted by Suicide

## Trish Nelson

A true story
of love, loss, survival and triumph

Edited by Beth Quinn

Copyright 2013, Trish Nelson

All Rights Reserved. No part of this publication may be reproduced, stored in or introduced into a retrieval system or transmitted in any form or by any means (electronic, mechanical, photocopying, recording or otherwise) without the express permission of the copyright owner.

E-mail: info@itwasnoaccident.com

ISBN: 978-1491267752

For My Luke and My Trisha
In Memory of Their Father

"... Lo and I am with you always,
even unto the end of the age."
～ Matthew 28:20

## Credits

Prologue and Epilogue by Beth Quinn
Chapter 11 by Trisha Nelson
Chapters 15 and 22 by Luke Nelson
Cover Design by Gerard Schaffner
Edited by Beth Quinn

# Contents

| | |
|---|---|
| Preface | i |
| Prologue | 1 |
| Howard | 17 |
| Trish | 21 |
| Life with the Lifeguard | 25 |
| Howard's Back | 41 |
| Paying It Forward | 47 |
| Saying Goodbye | 55 |
| Under the Microscope | 69 |
| Heading for a Breakdown | 75 |
| Grief Journal, The First Year | 81 |
| Teen Grief | 101 |
| Trisha Speaks | 109 |
| Grief Journal, The First Year, Con't | 113 |
| Be Calm, Eat Bacon, Believe in the Bear | 137 |
| Diesel And Daisy | 149 |
| Diesel's Story | 161 |
| People Say the Damndest Things | 167 |
| Grief Journal, The Second Year | 171 |
| Carnival Dating | 181 |
| Grief Journal, Onward | 189 |
| Gerard | 197 |
| Grown Up | 203 |
| Luke Speaks | 207 |
| No Lectures but a Bit of Advice | 215 |
| Why Didn't I Know What I Knew | 219 |
| Luke's Toast | 223 |
| Epilogue | 227 |

# Preface

Suicide.

Yup, that's how he died. No hiding it right from the beginning.

I think often of those families who have gotten the chance to hide a relative's suicide. How did they do that? Who, upon finding the dead person, had enough foresight to say right then and there, "I need to cover this up."

Part of me so wishes I could have done that when I found Howard in our bedroom, still alive with his eyes open, his chest rising and falling as he tried to breathe through the blood in his nose and throat. Part of me wishes I'd had the foresight to say, let me quietly exit, take the kids out of the house and call a policeman I know who might help make this look like an accident.

But obviously I couldn't do that. Why? Mostly because, from the moment I found Howard on our bedroom floor with half his head blown away, I remember thinking, "What happened here?" I could not figure it out. Not then, and only slightly better now.

The story I have been wanting to tell is about my life now, nearly six years after my husband killed himself. I have decided to write a book about me – not that I am so amazing or have had such an amazing life. I haven't traveled, I haven't won any awards nor have I discovered anything earth shattering.

I am just a fifty-one-year-old widow with two children. I was married only twenty years when my husband shot himself in our bedroom and I discovered him still alive. My kids and I have not only survived but have come out the other side whole.

*Howard*

Reasonably whole, anyway.

This book is about us. It's about Howard's death, his still-alive body and blood on the floor. It's about the events that led up to the bullet. I'll explain what he did and why he did it, to the extent that anyone can know what's really in someone else's mind at the moment he holds a .22 and places the gun directly onto his right temple and pulls the trigger.

Mostly, though, this book you're holding – or reading on a Kindle or a Nook or an iPad – is about how his suicide had, as you might imagine, just a teeny, tiny, little, itsy bitsy effect on his two teenaged children, his wife – me! – his neighborhood on Oxford Road, and even his town.

You will find some sadness in this book. And some anger. And some grief. And even some happiness. And while it's true that suicide is rarely funny – in fact, it's probably safe to say that suicide is never funny – you will also find humor in this book.

Life can be pretty grim, even for those who lead charmed lives without suicide or chronic pain or cancer or Alzheimer's or poverty or any of the other bad luck thrown our way that can sap the joy right out of us. And if you can't find a way to laugh, then you might as well just pull down the shades, lock the door, turn off the music, let the dishes get crusty with old food, let your hair go stringy and limp, let your bed sheets turn dingy and gray, and shuffle around in your rattiest slippers and bathrobe.

Because if you can't figure out what's funny, then you're dead now, too.

A couple of years ago, when my friends were all telling me, "You ought to write a book, Trish," I thought of a title. There was no book yet, but I thought I had a title.

My golden retriever, Diesel, was outside in a rain storm running from one side of the yard to the other. He was answering the thunder. Each time he heard it, he looked to the sky and barked right back at it, then ran to the other side of the yard. He seemed to be trying to have the last word, and he was confused that the sky seemed to have an answer for everything. Why wouldn't the sky just shut up after he'd told it to?

"You're never going to figure it out!" I yelled to Diesel. And I promptly told myself that if I ever wrote a book, which I doubted, I would title it, "You're Never Going To Figure It Out."

Well, the book is done now and, as you can see, that is not the title. Still, as I write this, I'm struck by the full force of the truth in those words. There are so many things I will never figure out.

I won't ever know why my husband's father felt it was better to take care of himself and others before his family. Why did my husband's smell always make me calm and long to just crawl up beside him? Why do teenage daughters take on an alien, harsh personality so that, no matter how much kindness and love you bestow on them, it never seems to fix things? Why do I long to be one of those widows whose husbands are long dead and who are moving on?

It is so much easier for me to talk a story than write one. I need to hear my voice, use my hands and see the reaction of others, especially in their eyes. Writing is solitary. There is no one there to react, and I've often thought, "For crying out loud, who would want to read this?"

It is in answering that question that I found the reason to keep writing. There must be other widows out there who will see themselves in my story and realize, "I'm normal!" after sharing my experience.

There must be survivors of a spouse's suicide who will read this and think, "Wow! Compared to this lady, I'm not doing too bad!"

There must be single women and men who have sought a new partner after being out of the dating world for decades who will recognize the frustration, fear, hilarity, depression, awkwardness and absolute confusion of my experience.

Yes, and there must be single parents who have to raise their children on their own after a spouse has died, and perhaps they will recognize themselves in my struggles.

I wonder, though, whether there are those as blessed as I am to have such an array of amazing family, friends, co-workers and even neighbors to help them through their tremendous grief and pain? Perhaps there are. I hope so.

I realize that, although my husband's suicide was a traumatic enough event to warrant a chapter or two here, what occurred after that suicide is what makes up the meat of this book: the cementing of a neighborhood in the wake of his death; the changed life of a woman who thought she would be married forever to the only man she had ever loved; the downhill slide into despair of two teenagers after their dad killed himself; and their mother's desperate attempt to pull them back to walk among the living again.

Who would want to read this book? I guess anyone who happens to be in such a situation. Or maybe just those closest to us on Oxford Road in Goshen, New York, and in our family and circle of friends.

I want them to know what happened after Howard killed himself, but I also want them to hear the story of the Howard I knew before it happened. And I want them all to know of the tremendous ways they have touched my life and the lives of my children, Trisha and Luke.

Mostly, I want to relay to the world what courage and character a twelve-year-old girl and a fourteen-year-old boy can summon from within to take on the world against all odds.

That, I discovered, is reason enough to write this story.

Trish Nelson<br>Summer 2013

# Prologue

## Memorial Day
## May 28, 2007

    As near as anyone on Oxford Road can recall, it was shortly before 5 p.m. when Trish Nelson came flying out of her house at No. 10 and stood screaming in the middle of the street.

    It was the end of Memorial Day weekend, and the street had been quiet until Trish's screams shattered the silence. Most people were in their back yards or inside their homes as the holiday wound down to a close.

    Craig and Sara Benson, who live next door to the Nelsons at No. 8 Oxford, were having a small, impromptu barbecue on their back deck with a couple of friends. One of their guests was a third-grade teacher in the village, Leigh Splendorio, who had stopped by with her fiancé.

    Craig and Sara can recall only a very few details of that small party. "I remember hot dogs," Sara said. Craig remembers beer. "I might have had four or five," he said. There was definitely beer.

The neighbors on the other side at No. 12, Scott and Danielle Brinkley, weren't home when Trish ran screaming into the street. Only moments earlier, Danielle and her three young boys had been sitting on their front stoop waiting for the ice cream truck, but it never showed up on Oxford Road that afternoon.

Danielle gave up, figuring maybe the truck had sold out at the parade downtown earlier in the day. But her sons were psyched for ice cream, so she called her husband on his cell and asked if he wanted to meet her and the kids at What's The Scoop, down on Matthews Street.

Scott doesn't remember where he was when he got his wife's call – maybe at the apartment complex just down the hill from Oxford, putting out a mulch fire with some of the other volunteer firefighters in the village.

That's where Howard Nelson's closest friend, Steve O'Sullivan, was. Fighting the mulch fire. Steve, who lives just around the corner from Oxford on Fletcher Street, is another volunteer firefighter. So was Howard. At least he was until the excruciating pain in his back became his constant companion.

But Scott just doesn't remember whether he was at the fire or not when Danielle called. He met his wife and kids at the ice cream stand, and that's where he was when he heard the 911 summons for help on his fire department pager.

"Medical assist needed on Oxford Road. Gunshot wound on Oxford Road."

Steve, down at the mulch fire, heard the summons on his pager, too. And they both just knew. It had to be Howard. They each ran to their cars and raced to Oxford from opposite directions.

Danielle took the kids to her parents. She had a real bad feeling about this.

Across the street from the Nelson house at No. 15, Mark and Meri O'Hara were sitting together on the glider in their back yard listening to WPDH. The radio station's annual countdown of the Top 100 rock songs was closing in on the final three, and Mark was wondering if "Stairway to Heaven" would be number one. "That's always the top song, so I figured it probably would be again," said Mark.

But Mark would not be anywhere near his radio by the time the number one song was announced.

Three doors down from Mark and Meri, at No. 9, Harry Mills was sitting at his computer. His desk was in the living room, just inside the front door. When he heard a knock, he barely had to get out of his chair to answer it.

"It was little Trisha," said Harry. Little Trisha Nelson, the twelve-year-old daughter of Trish and Howard. She was standing on his porch barefoot, banging on his door.

"Something's wrong with my father," Trisha told Harry. "I think my father's sick."

Harry yelled out to his wife Mary to call 911. Then he grabbed his slippers and ran out the door, leaving little Trisha behind with his wife.

"When I got outside, I saw Trish standing there in the middle of the street screaming," he said. "She had a cordless phone in her hand." The phone was smeared with blood.

"Howard shot himself!" Trish was screaming. "He shot himself!"

Harry ran past Trish, into her house and up the stairs. All he had to do to find Howard was follow the noise – a terrible, loud, wet snoring-like noise that he soon realized was Howard trying to pull in oxygen through the blood that had filled his throat and nose.

Craig Benson was already there, stunned at the sight of his friend and neighbor lying on the floor in a pool of his own blood, struggling to breathe. Mark O'Hara would soon join them. All three men saw the gun on the bed. Harry covered it with the bed sheet. And it was Harry who noticed a folded piece of paper on top of the tall dresser against the wall.

At No. 17, across the street from the Brinkleys, Beth and Bob Quinn don't recall what drew their attention to the street out front. It must have been Trish screaming but, really, they can't remember. Whatever it was, Beth opened her own front door and ran out into the street.

The next thing she remembers is sitting with Trish on the Brinkleys' front stoop, on the very spot Danielle had vacated moments earlier when she left for the ice cream stand. There was a man sitting on the other side of Trish – to this day, no one recalls who it was – and Trish was rubbing her hands together. Rubbing them, twisting and turning them.

Her fingers and palms were covered in her husband's blood. As she rubbed them together, the blood spread onto the backs of her hands, onto her wrists, onto her arms.

"I was afraid he'd do this," Trish wailed.

Two days earlier, she had asked Howard if he had thoughts of suicide. He said no, that he loved her and the kids. He'd never kill himself, he said.

Still, her fear had persisted. "This morning I told him, if you're thinking about killing yourself, Howard, please give me fifteen minutes to get help." She spoke as she watched her own bloody hands twist and turn in her lap. "I said please just talk to me first."

Howard apparently had nothing more to say. He was done talking. And so he held a .22 up to his right temple and pulled the trigger instead. No one on Oxford Road heard the gunshot.

\* \* \*

Oxford Road is not so much a road as a side street in the village of Goshen, New York, a street with about twenty modest homes built in the 1960s when the Ryerson Farm was sold to a developer. Many of those homes were enlarged and improved upon during the eighties and nineties when times were good. Additions were built, roofs were raised, new siding was installed, front porches and back decks were added. By the time the Nelsons bought No. 10 in 2002, the house had been transformed from a tiny ranch into a spacious split level.

From the outside, the Nelsons appeared to be a happy family except for Howard's back. Most everyone on the street knew Howard was depressed because of the constant pain. Nothing would touch it. Recent surgery had accomplished nothing. Pain pills were useless. Physical therapy was pointless.

"You could see it in his face, in how he walked," said Joe Bayno, who lives on the corner of Oxford and Fletcher. "I'd see him out walking those dogs every day, Diesel and Daisy. He'd have the dogs on a leash in one hand, and he'd be holding that tall walking stick of his in the other. He looked like an apostle coming down the street. A sad apostle. He couldn't do anything, he told me. He couldn't go to work, he couldn't take care of his house or yard, he couldn't sleep. He never slept, he told me."

Howard's back problems are a long story, but they began with driving big UPS trailer trucks with bad suspensions for more than twenty years. Bouncing around in those trucks on the night shift caused some bulging discs in his back, and two corrective surgeries not only failed to correct the problem, but they made matters worse. Nerve pain in the back. Terrible, never-ending nerve pain that grew steadily worse.

That whole Memorial Day weekend in the Nelson household was a grim one, at least as far as Trish was concerned. Howard barely got out of bed. He didn't talk much. Diesel, their golden retriever, and Daisy, the family's little spaniel mix, rarely left Howard's bedside.

"The dogs would come down for meals, they'd go outside to pee, then they'd go right back upstairs to be with Howard," said Trish.

By Monday afternoon, Trish was fed up. "I was aggravated," she said. "Howard wasn't getting up, he wasn't communicating. He had a bad headache, a terrible headache, but I couldn't convince him to let me take him to the hospital for help."

Trish went into nurse mode – she was the head nurse at Good Samaritan Hospital's dialysis unit at the time – and she began lecturing Howard about not stopping the pain pills all of a sudden like he was doing because he felt they were useless. And she was worried about the anti-depressants he was taking. The doctors had just put him on Paxil, along with Welbutrin, and she read her husband the side effects.

"I remember saying to him there's a risk of suicide with this," said Trish. "I said to him, if you're going to hurt yourself, talk to me. I'll have help here in fifteen minutes.

He said he'd never do that. He said he loved me and the kids too much."

Then she went into mommy mode. "The kids had been cooped up all weekend with a depressed father upstairs in bed," she said. "I said I don't know what the hell to do for Howard. I've got to take care of the kids." She decided to take Trisha and Luke to see an afternoon showing of *Pirates of the Caribbean II* at the Galleria in Middletown.

Luke, who was fourteen, doesn't recall feeling cooped up. In fact, the weekend had seemed pretty much like every other in recent memory.

"My father had his bad days in bed," said Luke. "This didn't seem any different. Right before we left for the movies, he asked me to make him a peanut butter and jelly sandwich. He liked how I made them on toast so the peanut butter would melt. I brought it up to him, and then we left."

Trisha didn't go upstairs to see her dad before leaving. "I just called goodbye up the stairs to him," she said. Just a normal goodbye, hollered up the stairs.

As she and the kids headed out, Trish didn't really give a thought to Howard's gun collection. That was something that had just always been there, passed down from Howard's father and added to over the years. Guns for hunting, guns for protection, guns for show. They were part of the household, like the furniture and lamps and kitchen knives.

She pulled out of the driveway and took her children to the movies.

The movie, said Luke, really sucked. None of them liked it, and it was way too long. Trish felt edgy and worried about Howard. She couldn't wait for it to end. Little Trisha remembers only one scene from the movie.

"The squid guy in the movie opened a jewelry box and it played a song – the same song the jewelry box my dad gave me plays," said Trisha. "I don't know the name of it. But when I heard that song, this feeling of terror washed over me. It felt like something was really wrong, but I didn't know what."

The feeling passed, and Trisha figured it was just the movie that had her creeped out.

* * *

Trish was the first one into the house when they finally got home, shortly before five o'clock. The kids followed her in.

"The first thing I saw was Diesel and Daisy," said Trish. "They were downstairs in the family room looking up at me as I walked in the door. They were penned in behind a child gate."

How weird, she thought. Even as she was trying to sort out why Howard had gotten out of bed and walked down two flights of stairs to lock up the dogs, she could hear the loud snoring-like sound, that wet gurgling noise, coming from upstairs.

"I took the stairs two at a time," said Trish. "When I went into the bedroom, Howard was lying on the floor between the dog crate and the bed. His back was arching. I thought he fell. I took his head and moved it. That's when I saw the right side of his head – it was completely blown open. There was a pool of blood under him, on the wall, on the dog crate. Blood was coming out of his nose, his mouth, out of everywhere. The gun was lying on the bed."

"I heard my mom upstairs yelling, 'Howard, what did you do, Howard?!'" said Luke. "Then she yelled, 'Call 911!'"

Luke started bounding up the stairs with the phone. He had dialed 911 but didn't know what to say. Trish ran from the bedroom and closed the door behind her. "Don't come up!" she told Luke. He tossed his mother the phone.

"Go get help!" she yelled to both kids. Trisha didn't know what for, but she ran across the lawn to Craig and Sara's and began pounding on their front door. She was barefoot, she said, and it would not be until the next day that she'd have a pair of shoes to put on.

Craig and Sara were out back barbecuing hot dogs. They didn't hear their twelve-year-old neighbor's knock. Trisha gave up and ran across the street to the Mills' house.

Trish told 911 to come fast. "I'm at No. 10 Oxford," she said. "I think my husband shot himself. Come quick!"

"The guy on the phone wanted to know who was in the house with me," said Trish. "I got mad. 'What are you doing, taking attendance? What the hell do you care who's here? Send an ambulance!'"

Then she ran out onto her own back deck and shouted over to Craig and Sara. "Howard shot himself!" Craig leaped the chain link fence between their back yards. "I asked Craig to go in with Howard," said Trish. Then she ran out into the street holding the blood-smeared phone and called her family. Her sister Kathy's husband Richie, who lived only a quarter-mile away on Golden Hill Avenue at the time, answered the call. He turned white when he heard Trish's screams. Then he dropped the phone, ran out of his house and headed for Oxford Road.

Harry Mills raced by Trish and entered her house. Luke ran across the street to the O'Hara house and knocked on the door. Mark and Meri's daughter Jen opened it. "Please get your mom," Luke told her.

Meri led Luke to her back yard. Mary Mills came rushing down the street with Trisha, and they joined Luke and Meri in the back yard. Mark crossed the street and entered the Nelson house, where Craig and Harry were already in the bedroom listening to Howard trying to breathe through the blood in his throat and nose. Harry pulled the sheet up over the gun.

Someone, a man – maybe it was Richie – led Trish to the Brinkleys' front porch, and Beth Quinn ran across the street to sit with them.

"It was just chaos," said Meri. "The street was suddenly filled with emergency vehicles – police, ambulance, fire trucks, everything with lights and sirens."

"I could hear what was going on out in the street," said Luke. "I got a glimpse of so many people and the fire trucks. People kept me in the back yard and tried to calm me down. I still didn't know what happened. No one that day told me what happened."

Trisha was mostly just so confused. Plus everyone kept asking her where her shoes were. "That went on all day," said Trisha. "It almost became a weird joke, people asking me where my shoes were."

What made the day even weirder for her – surrealistic, really, kind of like a strange dream – was when "all of a sudden our neighbor Sara came into Meri's back yard with my third-grade teacher, Miss Splendorio. I hadn't seen her in four years, not since third grade, and I was thinking things must be pretty bad if they called my third-grade teacher to comfort me. She was hugging me and patting me. None of it made any sense at all."

Trish's parents, Jack and Mary Kitson, suddenly materialized on the street. So did about fifty or sixty other people, including Steve O'Sullivan and Scott Brinkley.

"I had to fight with the fire police at the end of Oxford to let me get onto the street," said Scott. "I shouted, 'I live here! I live here! Let me past!'"

When he got to his driveway, he jumped from his car and literally climbed over the three people sitting on his porch. He grabbed Trish beneath the arms and hauled her into the house, with Beth and the unnamed man – maybe it was Richie – following.

"I remember Scott leading the three of us through his kitchen into the den," said Beth. "I saw that the sink was filled with dirty dishes and I had this wild, crazy thought that Danielle would be mad at Scott for letting us see the mess in the kitchen."

Scott handed Trish a glass of water and then went next door to see if he could help the EMTs. They were bringing Howard out. He was intubated and they'd wrapped his head up. The ambulance took off for the local hospital, Arden Hill.

The police came out of the house with Howard's guns. "There were so many," said Mark. "I couldn't believe how many guns Howard had. I had no idea."

The police also took the piece of folded paper that Harry had seen on top of the tall dresser in the bedroom. The house was, after all, a crime scene. It would be several days before they returned it to Trish. When they did, it was the first she knew that her husband had written a suicide note.

After the emergency vehicles and people left, "a group of us gradually came together on my front lawn," said Meri. "We just stood there staring at the empty house across the street. A couple of times someone spoke, but mostly we all just stood there. I just remember the silence. The whole street was so silent."

It was Scott who would go in and clean up the bedroom. He took in a bucket and sponge from his own house next door, and he washed Howard's blood and bits of brain and tissue off the wall and floor.

The next day, he would call Mike Nuzzolese at the village DPW and ask him to bring up the garbage truck to take away the mattress and box spring. "Trish didn't need to come home to that," said Scott. It wasn't Oxford Road's regular garbage day, but of course Mike came with the truck.

Terryl Delaney, the pastor at Trish's church, Grace Community in Washingtonville, arranged for the bed to be replaced. It would be there, all made up with new sheets and blankets, when Trish returned to her own bedroom two nights after her husband shot himself there.

\* \* \*

Trish has no idea how she got to the hospital, but she knows her brother Jimmy and her parents were with her. Steve O'Sullivan followed the family in his own car. The kids stayed behind at Meri's house. Eventually, they would end up at their Aunt Kathy and Uncle Richie's house, down on Golden Hill Avenue. They don't know how they got there.

"Everything is a blur at that point," said Trish. "Someone called Mona, my dog sitter. Maybe it was me, I don't know. But Mona came and got Diesel and Daisy. I didn't see them again for a few days, I don't think. Those poor dogs were totally traumatized. To this day, you can't crack your gum in the same room with Daisy without her getting spooked by the sudden noise."

The emergency room doctor told Trish there was no exit wound in Howard's head. The bullet was lodged behind his left ear. There might be a chance to save him, she was told.

Trish knew better. She's a nurse. And she knew that, even if they did save him, he'd be a vegetable the rest of his life. "Right then and there I said I don't think Howard shot himself in the head to live out his life as a vegetable, and I don't want that either," she said.

A helicopter arrived to transfer Howard to Westchester Medical Center in Valhalla. They offered to let Trish fly with them. Trish is nothing if not a pragmatist. "No," she told them. "I get air sick. You'll end up having to take care of me, too, if I fly."

Steve called the Goshen fire chief and said he needed the use of his car. He wanted lights and sirens all the way down. He headed for Valhalla with Trish and her parents, about a fifty-minute ride if you're going the speed limit. "I called ahead and told the State Police we were coming through." He doesn't know how fast he was driving, but no one got in his way.

"They'd already evaluated Howard by the time we got there," said Steve. "They had him on life support, and his brain was beginning to swell. Trish knew without being told. She knew Howard wouldn't make it. And she raised the issue of organ donation almost immediately."

"I told the E.R. doctor that I ran the dialysis unit at Good Sam," said Trish. "I said I knew quite a few people personally who needed a kidney."

Trish called Good Sam and talked to one of the nurses on duty in the dialysis unit. "Test everyone for a match," Trish told her. "I think we're going to have two available kidneys here."

"Then I remember looking at my parents and seeing my mother lean into my father," said Trish. "She said, 'Oh Jack, what are we going to do?' She was crying."

Trish remembers thinking, I know what I'm going to do. I'm going to tell the kids to start saying goodbye to their father.

* * *

No one told Luke what had happened that day. Not outright. He remembers watching *Mary Poppins* with his sister and younger cousins at his Aunt Kathy's house. "I remember thinking, will someone please shut this movie off," said Luke.

Trisha recalls very little from that evening except her Aunt Kathy asking where her shoes were. "I don't have them," Trisha said for maybe the fifteenth time that day.

Air mattresses were set up down in the family room for Luke and his mother, who was still at the hospital. Trisha wanted to sleep upstairs with her younger cousins, Rachel and Samantha. "I went to bed with Samantha's stuffed Tigger," said Trisha. "But I didn't sleep. Not right away."

When Trish got to Kathy's late that night — at least she thinks it was late, but who knows, really? — she told Luke his father might have had an accident and shot himself cleaning his gun.

"That's when I knew," said Luke. "My father taught me how to handle guns, and his big rule was, you never clean a loaded gun. Never. It was no accident."

"Aunt Kathy and my mother kept asking me if I wanted to cry," said Luke. "'Why aren't you crying, Luke?' they asked me. That made me angry. I didn't feel like crying."

Trisha heard her mom and brother and Aunt Kathy talking downstairs. She crept out of bed and went halfway down the stairs to listen. She could hear their voices but not their words. She sat there silently crying as she listened to their murmuring conversation.

"Then I just went back upstairs and got into bed with Tigger," said Trisha. "In the morning, Samantha and Rachel had to go to school. Samantha – she was only about seven years old – she had tucked her favorite stuffed horse into bed with me before she left for the bus. It was so unbelievably nice."

In the morning, Trish Nelson and her children went to their house to get some clothes. As they were leaving Kathy's house Trish asked her daughter, "Where are your shoes?" Trisha packed a couple of pair while they were home. Then Trish took her children to the hospital to visit their father.

Luke figured out on his own that his father wasn't going to make it. "When we went to the hospital that first day, I asked a nurse what this one machine was," he said. "She told me it measured the pressure in his brain. The first time we went, it was at 65 or 70. Each day we went, it was higher. It went into the 90s."

A machine was breathing for Howard. "At some point, after a few days, my mother told me, if he doesn't start breathing on his own tomorrow, it won't happen," said Luke.

He didn't. Howard was kept on life support until Thursday, May 31, 2007, three days after shooting himself. The doctors let him go after recipients were found for his kidneys, lungs, pancreas and eyes. They also harvested his skin, ligaments and tendons. The two men who received Howard's kidneys were Trish's patients in the dialysis unit. It didn't make her smile, but it felt hopeful in a small part of her soul.

And then Howard Nelson was gone.

* * *

For Oxford Road, Howard Nelson's suicide had come to an end. There would still be the wake and the funeral, of course, but the street quickly went back to its quiet, sleepy self. The neighbors didn't talk about Howard's suicide among themselves too much, at least not that summer.

For his widow and two children, though, Howard's suicide was just the beginning, the start of an alien new life without the man who had been their center, the man who had walked the dogs and who had sometimes stayed in bed all day and who had suffered such pain and who had loved them all so much.

"You know, my father and I didn't really get along all the time," Luke said. "We were usually mad at each other. But that day ... that was a good day for us. We weren't mad that day."

"And then that was it," he said. "That was it. That's all there was."

# 1

# Howard

I don't know which comes first, depression or alcoholism. Perhaps many people are depressed and self-medicate with alcohol. Or they drink and become alcoholics and then become depressed because of the drinking.

In Howard's case, I believe he self-medicated with alcohol to combat his depression. It wasn't a conscious decision, I'm sure. I doubt that, at the age of sixteen, he said, "Wow, I'm depressed and probably should be medicating myself – let me choose alcohol."

No, what most likely occurred is that he began drinking during his teen years and discovered that – for a little while, at least – he felt happier. Not joy, exactly, but less unhappy.

Howard was very competitive in sports during his adolescence, growing up in Chester, New York, during the 1960s and '70s. When he told me stories about his sports, his story-telling was always accompanied by a distant look and a set jaw. He was in no way going to sit the bench. He was determined to excel and he did, especially at baseball. But there didn't seem to be *joy* in this excelling. It was a duty, a mission, a chance to prove his worth and chase away his demons. My heart breaks as I write this because it is clear, in retrospect, that his soul was bruised even as a child.

I don't know if Howard suffered from depression prior to age ten. He told me very little about his childhood, but what he did tell me wasn't pleasant. He had parents who fought often and with no regard to the children in the house – Howard and his two sisters. He was the middle child.

His father was self-centered and created a home that revolved around himself. He was verbally abusive and unable to show empathy for his family, even though he was emotionally generous toward animals and strangers. He was smart but he lacked common sense. He was also a pack rat – he could have had a starring role on the show "Hoarders" if it had been around then – and his need to hoard continued until the day he died. Howard told me about some of his father's collections – items he basically took home from his job as a lineman for Orange and Rockland Electric. He never had enough. If he had twenty-five pairs of work gloves, he still needed twenty-five more – never to be used, only to be stored and claimed as his own.

He also had an apartment elsewhere – Howard thought it was in Rockland County, which is about 30 miles away – but no one spoke of this. Howard recalled meeting a woman who his father said was a friend. He said she was very nice to him.

Howard's grandmother doted on him when he was a child. He said she cared about him, and this memory seemed to both sadden Howard and make him happy. I remember his mother once telling me, "Howard was loved a lot," as though that was something unique in their family.

But maybe not so much. Birthdays in their house were not treated as special occasions. Holidays were noted but barely celebrated, and there was an undertone of annoyance at the intrusion in the daily routine caused by a holiday. The tone was set by both of Howard's parents. Anger, selfishness, hurtfulness, bitterness and abuse were the main ingredients in their home, and those emotions didn't take a day off just because it was a special day.

One of Howard's few happy childhood memories was of his mother's cooking. She was a great cook and the only time he became animated talking about his childhood was describing his favorite dishes. Then the poor guy married me, an Irish girl who was more interested in earning a living than cooking. I regret not cooking him one fabulous meal the entire time we were married. He was a better cook than I, by far.

Howard actually knew very little about his background. I remember thinking, how could he know so little about his relatives? His ancestors? Where they came from? What nationalities were in his lineage? Howard told me he never asked anyone. I wondered, how could anyone be so incurious about his place in the world?

He used to get mad at me for pressing him about his unhappy childhood. In angry moments, he would get defensive and say his family wasn't like mine – all crazy about everyone's birthday, wild at Christmas time, taking picture after picture. He acted as though such behavior is abnormal. But I also know his heart and soul ached for such love, kindness, support and just plain fun. Laughter, silliness, physical affection – Howard never had that.

And you know what? Some souls are so tender that the kind of environment he grew up in can wound deeply. Those wounds don't heal – they scar over, yes, but they remain just beneath the surface. Eventually they can open up again to destroy you. If life throws obstacles in your path, you can be defeated all the more easily. That, I think, is part of what happened to my Howard.

What sealed the deal for Howard was something that occurred when he was ten years old. I have struggled over whether to reveal his largest and most terrible life-long secret. Ultimately, I decided to include it here because it might help people understand what led Howard into the darkness he tried so hard to escape.

When he was ten, Howard went to stay with a friend on Long Island for a weekend. The friend's father molested Howard. While it was happening, the other boy stood there watching what his father was doing to him. As Howard struggled against his rapist, his friend told him, "It's okay! It will be over with soon!"

Afterward, Howard called his parents and asked them to come get him. He did not tell them why, and they said no. Howard hitch-hiked home from Long Island to Chester by himself. At age ten. He never spoke of it until we'd been married for several years. During those first years of our marriage, I often told him that he seemed so burdened by something. I asked him to please let me help, to please tell me what it was.

He didn't for ten years.

Then one day, during a particularly difficult time in our marriage, as he was leaving for work at 2:20 in the afternoon, I said to him, "What the hell is wrong? I know you carry something, and it is killing you – and us."

Howard suddenly blurted it out. His friend's father had molested him when he was ten years old.

In an instant, I was staring at that young boy who was finally telling someone about this most terrible thing for the first time. I dropped to my knees. How in God's name could someone do that to a boy? How could his parents not pick him up? How could he have survived thirty years carrying that inside him? What was I going to do to help him heal?

I cannot say much more about it. It explains a lot of Howard's dark moods, violent nightmares and isolation from me and others. He once told me, "I hate people." I finally knew why.

Howard was a good man with a kind soul who carried with him a wound so vicious and destructive that I sometimes marvel that he lasted as long as he did. He was a grown man, but he was also that ten-year-old boy who carried a burden of pain and guilt. He forever blamed himself.

I grieve for that boy. I cry each time I think of him, more than I cry for my fifty-two-year-old Howard who took his own life. For it all started with that child – a child no one watched out for.

# 2

# Trish

My own childhood, well ... that is a whole different matter.

I was born in 1962, the middle child of five to Irish Catholic parents in the Bronx. My first real memory is of the Great Northeast Blackout in 1965 when I was three years old. I remember my mom folding laundry in the dark with my Aunt Patsy. My Uncle Jimmy came by and ate the remainder of our stew. My dad was out fighting fires (and probably looters) for the FDNY.

My father is a born story teller – yes, many times we have heard the stories, but never do we tire of his tales of growing up in the Bronx; of the ice man and of selling bottled soda and then redeeming the empties; of his friend in Sing Sing; of joining the Marines at age seventeen and getting blown out of a bunker in Korea; of his days and nights with the fire department; of meeting my mom on a group date (only she was another guy's date).

My early childhood in the Bronx has given me some stories to tell as well: of the Christmas parties at Ladder 37 on Briggs Avenue; of visits to Throgs Neck to see my mother's family – Grandpa and Grandma Hosford and my aunts and uncles; of visits to Grandpa and Grandma Kitson where we kids were always served Coke in glasses with ice cubes and where bacon and skinny pretzel sticks were always on the table. The Hosford house had the sweeter treats – my brother Jimmy and I began our life-long love affair with Circus Peanuts at the candy dish in their living room.

It was from our home on Claflin Avenue in the Bronx that Grandpa Kitson walked me to kindergarten; where Jimmy and I sneaked up to the roof on the elevator only to look over the edge and discover my Dad looking up at us; where the basement "meter room" had a sump pump that Grandpa Kitson told me had snakes and huge water bugs swimming in it so I'd stay away from it; and where there was often a pervasive smell of fish head just outside the front door during the summer – apparently an old Jewish man thought it would help our front stoop garden grow grander if he planted some fish heads in it.

During the summer of 1968, my mom was mugged along the side of our building. The elderly black gentleman from across the street was the only one to risk his safety to come to her aid. It was this incident that got my parents thinking about moving us five kids out of the city to safer territory. A year later, we found ourselves living in a three-hundred home development in Chester, New York, called Surrey Meadows. The move took us

*The Kitson kids. Front, l-r, Kathy, Ann and Jimmy. Back, Trish and Johnny.*

sixty miles from the Bronx, but it might have well been six thousand miles.

My parents, no doubt, missed the city although my father still spent a lot of time in the Bronx for his shifts at the firehouse.

But us kids? There was nothing more fun than Surrey Meadows. On our street alone, there were more than fifty-five kids in twenty-three homes.

Most of our homes had one TV, one and a half bathrooms, and one phone with a very long cord that could stretch out of the kitchen, down the hallway and into the coat closet where we could talk in private. Outside, there was always a crowd playing wiffle ball, ring-o-levio and touch football or swimming in an endless sea of above-ground pools.

Christmas was always a big celebration in our home. My dad spent December rigging up unusual Christmas light configurations. For a few years, we had live music playing in the front yard with a spotlight highlighting the eighteenth century singers he had fashioned out of plywood. I honestly don't remember much about the gifts I received, but I do remember the smells and the feelings of joy that the holidays brought into our lives. I remember putting up the tree; the bendable elves we wrapped around the banister rungs; the stable that Grandpa Hosford made; putting baby Jesus in the manger *after* midnight on Christmas Eve; and the sight of my parents sound asleep in their room while a few small feet ventured down the hall to peek under the tree.

It was a far cry from the childhood Howard had endured.

\* \* \*

I actually remember meeting Howard when I was twelve years old and he was nineteen. He was one of two lifeguards at the Pius XII "bad boys" school, where we kids went on day trips during Chester rec camp. There was an Olympic-sized pool with both a high dive and a low diving board. Not only was the pool incredibly cool, so was the lifeguard named Howard.

It was during lunch break one day that I met him. He came up to me and pointed at my half-eaten sandwich. "Are you going to finish that?" he asked me. It was a plain baloney sandwich on Wonder Bread. Of course I wasn't going to finish it – I would have given that handsome teenager *all* of my lunches for the rest of the summer if he'd wanted them.

I don't believe he ever said another word to me that summer, and I never saw him again until five years later when I was a full-fledged teenager myself. I was hanging out at "the corner" – this was the corner in Surrey Meadows where Park Drive meets Surrey Road.

My girlfriends and I claim we founded this hangout, but I am not sure. No matter. It became The Corner in Chester during the late seventies and early eighties, and most local teenagers knew exactly what you meant when you said, "I'll be at the corner tonight."

It was such a crucial place for hanging out that I even had a punishment in the summer between ninth and tenth grade involving *not* being allowed to go to the corner. I imagine many kids my age smoked their first cigarette, drank their first beer and got kissed for the first time at the corner.

The owners of the house on that corner had a wide, long lot so we weren't exactly on top of their house. Still, they were very tolerant of the crowd that hung out on the side of their property most weekend nights. Their rustic wooden fence was great for sitting on, but we mostly sat on the curb or on the cars that stopped by.

I distinctly remember Howard pulling up in an El Camino one warm summer night when I was sixteen. One of his friends was in the car with him. He spoke briefly to one of the guys with us and then they were off. I remember thinking, "How do you get to be so cool?"

It would be another five years before I saw him again.

# 3

# Life With the Life Guard

The next time I met Howard, I was twenty-two years old. He was twenty-nine. Until then, I hadn't dated seriously. I just hadn't met anyone, and I didn't have much confidence.

Howard was kind and he seemed to need me, and I gravitated toward that need. I was so taken with him – his large frame, his quiet strength, his easy demeanor and gentle soul. We met while we were both playing in softball leagues. I was on summer break from Mount Saint Mary College, working at Key Bank in Chester and spending my free time playing in three softball leagues.

There were two fields side by side, the ladies' field and the men's. On Saturdays, all teams would be sitting in the stands with their coolers. Yes, we had beer in those coolers and had no problem drinking them before, during and after the games.

Howard's team was there on Saturdays, too. Howard was an outstanding ball player, a pitcher with endless potential. He could easily have been a professional baseball player. His fast ball was once recorded at ninety-eight miles per hour. If he'd had direction and support from capable adults, he could have landed in the major league, but he never received much of that. He ultimately broke the second finger on his pitching hand while playing at Orange County Community College, and he said that hurt his chances of ever going anywhere professionally.

I'm not too sure that was the only reason.

But it was because of softball that Howard and I met for the third time in our lives – five years after our last encounter. This time, we were both grown-ups. My friend Denise and I were sitting in the stands drinking mimosas when Howard approached us after the men's game ended. He invited us both to join him for dinner at the Alpine, a lonely Italian restaurant sitting on the side of the road between Chester and Washingtonville.

We said yes. We had no other plans and, well, I still remembered that cool life guard I'd met years ago. Denise was interested in another guy in Howard's circle, a man named Rick whom she eventually married.

Our dinner was funny, awkward and entertaining. Howard had recently separated from his wife and would soon be moving into an apartment in Middletown with a friend named Dutch. I tucked that information away, along with one other thing. He called me a cute little darling. I especially liked the *little* part.

Eventually it would become *my* cute little darling.

About a week after our dinner, when I was jogging and running hills at the Chester High School, there was Howard again, smiling as he strolled over to me.

"There's that cute little darling," he said to me by way of greeting. I was thrilled, nervous and flustered, but deep down I had a comfortable feeling, almost a "this is what I've been looking for" feeling.

But Howard, although separated, was still married. Not only that, he had three daughters, all under the age of seven. I was a young Catholic woman with no experience, and I had no idea how this was to work. Was it even legal to date someone separated? In the church's eyes, he was still married. Who should I ask?

My doubts were put to rest quickly by some girlfriends of mine when I asked their opinion of my dating Howard. They said, "What? We thought you two were already dating!" I figured if everyone already thought we were together and no one seemed to object, we might just as well do it.

He certainly wasn't the ideal man my family would have picked for me, though – a separated man living with another grown man in an apartment, paying alimony and child support for three children, Tara, Selina and Heather (girls as beautiful as their names).

Howard saw his girls only every other weekend. He often said he was a lousy father who didn't have a clue how to be a good one. I told him to mirror the actions of fathers like my dad, men who were good at it. I have no idea whether or not he tried to do that.

I do know that he loved his girls more than he ever told them and more than he ever showed them. He missed out on so much with them as a result.

We got engaged eighteen months after we began dating. If my family and friends had doubts about his suitability, they were quickly put to rest. Everyone really liked Howard. What was not to like?

He worked very hard at his job driving for UPS, and he worked equally hard at his hobbies.

He had a dry sense of humor that was always tinged with kindness. If he poked fun at someone, that person felt special, not hurt.

He was not prone to outbursts or strong anger.

He thoroughly enjoyed the company of animals, especially dogs.

He never overslept, even after getting only a few hours of sleep.

He was always ready and willing to lend a helping hand to a neighbor, acquaintance, stranger or the local fire company.

It was easy to like Howard and easy to be in his company.

What wasn't easy for me, though, was getting Howard to connect on anything other than the surface level. I wouldn't know why until I learned his terrible secret. The worthlessness he felt after being raped as a child permeated every aspect of his life. How could it not?

But I had no knowledge of this for the better part of thirteen years of trying to figure him out. It was exhausting and exasperating, and it was most often central to any struggles we had as a couple right from the start.

\* \* \*

I finished my bachelor's degree in communications from Mount St. Mary College before we were married. Howard was very proud of me. He often said how smart he thought I was, which I found so odd. He was the one who could read a full set of instructions and build what was meant to be built. I, on the other hand, could read, yes; but I had no talent for following directions or finishing a project.

*Trish and Howard*

Howard had inherent talent and smarts. I had book learning.

Our first five years together were spent being a couple. We moved from a basement apartment to an awesome house near Chester, in the Village of Florida; we spent time with his daughters; we went to my family's events and celebrations; we drank and spent time with friends; we played ball. We pretty much carried on as we had when we were dating.

I wasn't so sure about my job, though. I was traveling to New York City, more than a two-hour commute each way, to work in the public relations department of a major stock company. It was an exciting job, but the commute was exhausting.

I wondered how I could ever have children with such a long work day and with Howard working nights for UPS. We needed two salaries whether we had children or not, and I began to consider other options.

I literally woke up one morning and said to myself, "I'm going to be a nurse." This was odd because I had never taken care of anyone sick and really had no idea what a nurse did. Still, I knew without doubt that I needed to be a nurse.

I quit my job and enrolled in college to get my nursing degree. This was one of the best times for Howard and me. We were doing okay emotionally. I started cleaning houses to supplement our income, which was great work for me. Cleaning has always been therapy for me. I *love* to get in, get it done and step back to see just how great things look.

Howard not only worked at UPS during this period, but he also worked for the Village of Florida every day from 7 a.m. to 4 p.m. He survived on four hours of sleep a day.

I finished the nursing program in two years. The day I graduated, I started working at Good Samaritan Hospital. Finally, we could move forward knowing we could start a family and pay our bills.

\* \* \*

I became pregnant two years after starting work at Good Sam. We had bought our first home in Goshen at 93 Montgomery Street two months earlier. There, we happily discovered something we both enjoyed doing together – gardening. Howard preferred to call it landscaping, but … whatever.

Regardless of what we called it, we were both very good at it. Howard learned how to trim trees, often climbing very tall trees with spike straps on his legs and a saw and rope in hand.

The guy loved this type of work. I believe it allowed him quiet, uninterrupted time away from his pain and life in general, just like hunting did. Up in a tree, he could simply be Howard –no memories to contend with, no emotional trauma to deal with. Just a guy in a tree.

And I was pregnant.

But our brief period of contentment ended with a miscarriage at week seventeen of my pregnancy. We were devastated. It was so unexpected and, yes, it was a death. I was just plain sad.

Howard withdrew as he had many times when things got dark for him. We both retreated for a few months into our own interior worlds. Howard, who drank nearly every weekend as a matter of course, began drinking more heavily.

That fall and winter were dark and lonely. Howard began spending more and more time in the basement.

I got pregnant again. I was due in November 1992, and this time the nausea and tiredness seemed to be signs that, yes, I would keep this pregnancy. I never felt so good! I continued to run and work out as I had for the past ten years. Howard seemed to have a renewed sense of hope, and his drinking decreased a little.

Luke Nelson was born November 11, 1992, at 3:33 p.m. What a lazy baby! He hadn't moved around much in utero and he took nearly three hours to enter the world. But he smiled. Boy, did he smile! He lit up a room and lit up his parents' lives like never before.

That first year with Luke was almost magical. I loved being a mom and I think Howard finally got to practice being a real dad for the first time. He laughed a lot with Luke that year, and Luke laughed along with him. The house was alive.

Thirteen months later, I was pregnant again. Howard worried about supporting another child. I didn't. I was thrilled. I can't explain it, but the desire for another child was so very strong that fall. That Christmas, we announced my second pregnancy with an *I Love My Grandparents* bib to my parents.

*Howard and Luke*

Seven weeks into this pregnancy, I took a walk down the street to the Kwik Stop with Luke in a baby backpack carrier. I loved that thing. My arms and hands were free, and Luke had a great view of the world around him.

When we got home, I discovered I was bleeding. Again. Just like the first pregnancy. I was distraught. It was a Sunday, so I was instructed to lie down and keep my feet elevated until

Monday morning's doctor visit. I did as I was told but bled throughout the night.

We anticipated that the doctor would tell me I was miscarrying, that there would not be another baby.

The vaginal sonogram took longer than usual. The technician left and came back several times, which was unusual. Finally, I was instructed to get dressed and go into the doctor's office.

"You're miscarrying," the doctor told me. "But there's another one on the other side of your uterus."

I was pregnant with twins. I was losing one of them but not the other. Our emotions ran the gamut from sadness to relief, bewilderment to joy.

That pregnancy ended five weeks earlier than it was supposed to, on August 10, 1994, with Trisha Mary Nelson arriving at 2:18 a.m., just eighteen minutes after her mom arrived at the hospital. Her dad walked in just our baby girl entered the world.

My tiny Trisha weighed exactly five pounds and sported the scrawniest of chicken legs and arms. But she was the image of me. We had planned to name her either Bridget or Colleen, but we took one look at "mini-me" and decided she looked too much like a Trisha to be called anything else.

*Howard and Trisha*

The next two years were thrilling, but busy and tough to be sure. I went back to work full time when Trisha was only seven weeks old. A friend in Goshen babysat for Luke and Trisha. There was a mom, dad and two children in that house, and my kids loved it. Even at one year old, Trisha had a major crush on the dad, who would get Trisha laughing wildly. My kids had smiles on their faces every day when I picked them up.

During this time I worked days at the hospital as an educator in dialysis. Howard worked nights. He rarely slept more than four hours, even though he didn't have a second job to go to. I probably should have worried about him, but there wasn't time.

*Luke and Trisha*

\* \* \*

Something was changing in Howard. He was growing more withdrawn, spending more time down in the basement. Even when we were in the same room, he was just not with us. He was loving and kind with the kids, but he was often just not present.

And I noticed his weekend drinking was picking up again. It started Saturday when he woke up and continued through Sunday afternoon. He never drank during the week at all; he would never jeopardize his job.

There was a distinct change in him after he had a few drinks. First, he was much more talkative. Later, when the alcohol wore off, he grew angry and agitated.

I began to tell him I thought he had a drinking problem. I was often asking him, what's wrong? It seemed he was mad, angry, frustrated all of the time. What was it? Did he need to get counseling?

It was beginning to have its effects on our marriage, and I started looking into help for myself. I had been raised Catholic but felt something was missing and I was in need of some other kind of support. I needed help to find out how to get this right. How do I alleviate my growing sadness? I needed something beyond the Catholic Church to help me find my way. I began attending a Baptist church, Grace Community, where I was welcomed and where I felt closer to God.

Howard, too, tried to find ways to combat his growing depression and sadness. He joined the Minisink Fire Department in Goshen. He was so happy at the firehouse taking care of the tanker as a truck steward and completing training with his friend, Steve O'Sullivan, and others. These were important friendships – adult friends, not people from his past who were so tightly wound up in memories of his sad childhood.

But as I would come to learn, even though Howard excelled at being a fireman and loved it, this diversion like all others could not keep him from his depression. It would always come back.

* * *

I have a picture of Trisha when she was two years old. In it, she and her father are on the lawn at my sister Kathy's house. It is early summer, and Howard looks run down, distant and angry in the picture.

We had tried some counseling and, while it helped in small ways, the main problem remained –Howard's drinking and depression. Without question, I could have used some self-improvement, too, but not much progress can be made when an addiction is in the way.

There was never a time that I thought Howard didn't want to fix things. He did, but I think he thought it was impossible. I tried often to tell him that even little steps were worth their weight in gold. Just to try get counseling, take some medications, talk to someone. After each talk, we would connect for a while, and therein lay my ray of hope – I would grab that and hang onto it for dear life.

Then things would go back to where they had been. He would retreat and distance himself, Eventually, we would have "the talk" again. I could have saved myself years of trouble by taping that conversation and just hit "Play" when things got bad.

Odd events were starting to occur that I just couldn't quite get a handle on, but I knew they meant Howard was getting worse.

There was the time my parents said they went to the house to see the kids. I was working, and Howard was home with them.

My parents crossed paths with Howard as he was driving in the car with Luke. But … no Trisha.

My parents mentioned it to me, in passing really. I asked Howard about he. He said he just took Luke for a ride while Trisha was asleep.

At home. Alone. A two-year-old. I felt as if I'd been punched in the stomach. For crying out loud, who leaves a two-year-old home alone? Who in their right mind? Luke told me they "went to the store." I didn't ask Luke if Daddy had bought beer. I didn't want to drill my son, but I tucked it away.

Down at the shore, when we were eating out one evening, it seemed Howard had a few too many but it was difficult to know for sure sometimes. But his extremely rude encounter with a waitress because our food was taking longer than expected certainly suggested he was drunk. Howard was never rude to anyone outside of the house and definitely not in a public forum.

There were the empty beer cans stashed down in the basement; always in the basement. There were mood swings from euphoric to sullen and angry. None of this was a sign that things were improving.

There was a party at my Aunt Dotty's house in Middletown. I took the kids on my own and told Howard to join us if he wanted. It was growing very common for me to go to events alone with the kids. Sometimes Howard came; other times he didn't.

This time, Howard came. He was drunk. No one else noticed, but I did. We stayed for a while, but I spoke to Howard outside.

"I can tell you've been drinking," I told him.

"I only had two beers," he said. How many times did I hear that? How many times did I want to believe it? Two could have been one or twenty, it didn't matter – he always said he had two.

I watched as Howard swayed a little. I told him I was leaving the party. Trisha was already outside with us, and I went inside to get Luke and say some goodbyes. When I got back outside, I couldn't believe what I was seeing. Howard had put Trisha into his Jeep Cherokee and was driving away.

I threw Luke into the car seat and followed Howard. As I watched my husband driving drunk, I saw him barely miss a stop sign as he went off the road, then swing the vehicle the other way, barely missing an oncoming car.

By some miracle, he made it home with me right on his tail.

It was that night that I stopped bargaining with him. The kids were not safe with him on weekends, and nothing more was negotiable. If he wanted to continue living in the house, he would have to get help for his alcoholism and his depression, I said. Either AA or rehab, I told him.

He agreed. He would go to rehab, he said.

I told him to call UPS human resources first thing Monday morning.

Accessing a thirty-day rehab through the Employee Assistance Program at your workplace comes with conditions. Yes, UPS was fully supportive of this long-time employee who was admitting he had a drinking problem. But in the end, it is the company laying out close to $30,000 for the rehab and they fully expect the employee to adhere to the program.

I don't think Howard fully considered this. I think he just heard "thirty days away" and had a feeling of relief. I thought he might not fully realize what he'd agreed to until he checked in, and I was right.

Three hours after Howard got there, he sneaked a call to me. He was not supposed to call for the first five days, but there he was on the phone, three hours in.

He said he loved me and that he finally understood how serious his drinking was impacting things and that he'd learned a lot. (Really? In three hours?)

He said he was ready to come home and try harder. He would go to AA meetings and counseling.

I had to tell Howard that no, he couldn't come home. He really couldn't. He had voluntarily signed in using his company's money and would lose his job if he signed himself out.

Howard explained to me that he "wasn't like these people."

I hung up on him.

I went to family meetings at the rehab each Saturday. I brought cards from the kids and some approved goodies. Eventually, we were allowed to speak on the phone each night.

Howard worked the program and was very well liked. Of course. He was pleasant, cooperative and easy going. I doubt his participation went anywhere near to telling the truth or any deeper than just below the surface.

Howard was discharged thirty days later. At his discharge meeting, I was informed at great length by the rehab professionals that, going forward, this had to be about *Howard* – his sobriety, his emotions, his counseling all had to come first; before our relationship, before me, before the kids.

We had to operate our lives and our family around whatever Howard needed to remain sober and work the program. My blood began to boil.

I am not an alcoholic, so I don't know the struggles of attempting to live a sober life. What I *do* know is how damn hard it is to a) live with an alcoholic and b) live with an alcoholic who is working the program and trying to stay sober.

This disease is selfish and, as I came to find out, so is the recovery. I was furious. I told them that the last nine years had been about Howard and that, quite frankly, with two little kids at home and a full-time job, I didn't have the time to make sure everything was about him.

We left with me driving. In all the twenty-three years I knew Howard, there was never a time I was angrier with him than during that ride home.

He reached over and said, "You know I love you," and I just blew. I screamed, yelled, cried – everything I probably should have let out much earlier and much more slowly over the years.

I was enraged and distraught, and I didn't know where to put it all.

\* \* \*

Howard was home two weeks before he drank again.

He went to maybe three AA meetings in those two weeks. He also went to an outpatient counselor. I went with him once and, trust me, this "certified alcohol counselor" wasn't sober. I could smell the alcohol on him.

Howard used to say I could smell the alcohol off of a year-old beer cap three miles away. I said no, I just paid attention. And this guy was hitting the bottle between sessions. Howard went to this "counselor" for a year. He drank that entire year, on weekends and vacations.

I was at the end of my rope and had to make a decision. Do I stay and live this life, or do I tell Howard to move out? After a serious talk with my sister-in-law Diane and my pastor, I realized that I didn't want the marriage to end. I loved Howard and had a responsibility to stay and work on the parts I could make better. And he was the father of Luke and Trisha. I didn't want them to live without their dad.

And I could pray – pray that God would ease Howard's pain and addiction and that I could remain solid and supportive for as long as he needed me to.

It was a good decision.

Howard drank for another year, but he also started attending Grace Community Church with me and the kids that year. Little by little he started listening, and little by little I saw something crack. He now shed tears instead of anger. It became common to see Howard cry silently during a service and hold my hand. Then he would give Pastor Terryl a big bear hug on his way out.

Finally, there came the afternoon when Howard told me about being raped as a child. To the best of my knowledge, and I have a good nose, Howard never drank again.

\* \* \*

It was early 2001. Luke was nine and Trisha was seven, and I began dreaming of a bigger house on a nicer street for us.

I had been working at Good Samaritan for eleven years, and Howard had been with UPS for twenty-one years. We were making decent money.

By August, I wasn't exactly house hunting yet when I happened to see a house for sale on Oxford Road, which is an awesome street in the village – a great street for kids to play, a fenced-in yard, a nice-looking home with a recent addition. I was in love!

Howard was very skeptical. My goodness, this place was $225,000. Who pays $225,000 for a house? But I knew – I just knew this was *our* house.

One month later, on September 11, 2001, the Twin Towers fell and thousands were killed. It seemed that no one looked at any houses at all that fall and winter. But in early 2002, I convinced Howard to put our Montgomery Street house up for sale and see what happened.

It worked out. By June, our old house was sold, and we bought the Oxford Road house. Soon afterward, housing prices went wild in the Village of Goshen and elsewhere in Orange County. It seems that everyone wanted to move a safe distance away from New York City.

I have a picture of Luke and Trisha going to school that September of 2002. They are standing on the steps of 10 Oxford Road, both with newly cut hair, brand new shorts, shirts, book bags and lunch boxes. They are so very happy, healthy, strong and full of life.

Our neighbors were having babies; the Brinkley twins were nine months old. There was so much life on that street and so much to be thankful for. Howard and I and our family were in a great place.

I was thrilled to be in a house that felt like a home, and we worked on a little by little. I decorated, planted, painted, rearranged. We put in a new kitchen and bought an above-ground pool.

Howard and I spent many evenings sitting on those three front steps together watching Luke and Trisha play in the street. Sometimes we joined them in a game of around-the-world basketball, tossing a softball, kicking a soccer ball, throwing a Frisbee.

As the toddlers on the street grew, they'd join in as best they could. The little ones worshipped Trisha and Luke.

Our first three years in that house, from 2002 to 2005, were the most fun, loving, romantic and exciting time Howard and I had together. He never drank anything but O'Douls. We were working hard and getting ahead. The kids were doing well in school taking part in after-school and community activities We were all going to Grace Community Church as a family.

Life was full and we were blessed.

Howard was a true romantic in our early years as many men are, and his demonstrations of love continued throughout most of our years together. He used to say we were soul mates long before those words were popular. He said "you got me," and I always felt accepted, protected, loved and secure with him by my side.

He often surprised me with presents of jewelry, cards and silly things to make me laugh.

He brought me flowers until about a year before he killed himself.

At Christmas, he wrapped the presents he bought for us even though wrapping wasn't exactly his forte. There was nothing funnier than watching the kids unwrap gifts that had enough paper on them to cover a mall's worth of presents.

\* \* \*

But that fabulous, happy time when we were all so in love was to come to an end, and so very abruptly.

I believe the beginning of the end started with Chili, the very first dog we owned as a family.

Chili was a golden retriever we bought from a backyard breeder. At the time we bought her, we didn't know that her mother was a nervous, hysterical, nippy wreck.

We met Chili around Halloween of 2004, and she was eight weeks old when we took her home. The kids immediately fell in love with her. So did Howard and I.

Chili quickly grew to love us in return, but that love soon turned to obsession, especially with Trisha and me. This led to very aggressive behavior as she wanted to protect us from *everyone*.

I will never forget the day our neighbor Danielle came into our yard to pet her. Chili stood between Trisha and me. It was the first time I'd ever witnessed a dog curl its lip up and show its teeth.

I remember looking down at Chili and thinking, "My God, could she be smiling? Do dogs smile?" It didn't register that curling her lip and showing her teeth was a serious sign of aggression, but I tucked the incident away.

The next episode came when Trisha's friend Jordan was at the house – someone who had known Chili since she was a pup. This time the curled lip turned into a snap at Jordan's hand. She missed but I felt an alarm go off in my head. Something wasn't right with this dog.

I brought her to the vet who agreed that something seemed off. She was an extremely nervous girl with such in-born fear! The vet suggested an anti-depressant.

From there, I tried everything. I tried special dog food, extra walks, herbal supplements, a costly trainer. I even spent $1,000 to take Chili to a dog psychologist, who agreed that something was neurologically amiss with her.

Then Chili began attacking other dogs. First, it was my neighbor's ten-year-old, overweight Labrador – a vicious attack on a sweet, docile dog. Something was terribly wrong. I began making sure the kids were never alone with her, and their friends were not allowed to pet her.

That summer, we left Chili with the trainer for a week when we went to the shore. While we were gone, I got a call. Chili had attacked another dog. The vet bill was $700.

I knew then what I had guessed for months and had tried to prepare Howard for. We would have to put her down. Howard begged me to let him keep her in the backyard tied up, but that would have been a terrible life for the dog. And it was only a matter of time before she would move on from attacking other dogs to attacking people.

Howard took her to the vet. We were all devastated.

After Chili was put down, it seemed that Howard's health began to decline. His depression came back and, along with his back pain, it soon took over Howard's life.

Nothing was ever the same after that.

Still, I never thought he would desert us the way he did.

# 4

# Howard's Back

I sometimes think of Howard as "Howard's back." His bad back was so intricately woven into the fabric of who he had become by the time he killed himself that sometimes I can hardly see him in my memory as anything but back pain.

By the time Howard got to that point, though, he had worked for thirty years as a driver for UPS. For twenty of those years, he drove tractor trailers, often times doubles, hundreds of miles a night while I was home with the kids. We spent most of our marriage working opposite shifts to save on child-care costs.

In addition to driving those tractor trailers, Howard was an outdoorsman. He thrived on heavy physical labor and hard work. He climbed trees, he hauled whatever needed to be hauled, he lifted heavy equipment even if it weighed far more than his own strapping 230 pounds. At 6'3" he was a solid, handsome man.

His love for the outdoors sent him into the woods. He was an avid hunter and spent every fall in the woods, most often up in a tree where he would sit for hours in the damp, freezing cold. This would put stress on the strongest of backs.

Perhaps all of his physical activity would not have been so damaging had he been employed in an easier profession. Year after year, he'd bounce around in those trucks that he said had no suspension whatsoever. He drove steadily, safely and conservatively, but there was no escaping the long shifts of bouncing around in those trucks.

Over the years, Howard's back pain grew to be his constant companion. It was at its worst after times of inactivity, when he tried to get out of bed or a chair or his truck. It wasn't uncommon to come home and find him lying flat on his back on the floor with the kids and a dog around him. It slowly, inexorably grew worse.

Finally, he confessed he needed help and toward the end of 2003 – about four years before his death – I sent him to a chiropractor. In hindsight, I ask myself why I didn't make him go see a neurosurgeon first. And why didn't I send him to New York City, which is only sixty miles away and has some of the finest specialists in the world? Why didn't I force the issue?

The chiropractor was a nice enough person, and he seemed competent. The visits went reasonably well for a few months. But then there was that day – it was in May 2004 – the very last day Howard went to the chiropractor and the day he began a steady decline.

He had numbness down his right leg that day and a stabbing pain in the low back, mostly on the right side. He was heading to work in late afternoon, and he stopped in to see the chiropractor on his way.

The chiropractor was much smaller than Howard, easily six inches shorter and maybe seventy pounds lighter. He told Howard to lie on his left side with his left leg under him and his right leg bent up towards his chest. His arms were crossed.

That's when the chiropractor jumped onto Howard's hip. Why? Who knows? Maybe it was an attempt to pop a disc into place? Whatever his goal, it didn't work. And so he jumped onto Howard's hip again – and then it happened. There was a pop, yes, but something else happened, too. There was a very loud, ominous noise – the sound of something that should *not* have happened.

The chiropractor wondered out loud what that noise was. He had a puzzled look on his face – something you never want to see on the face of a health-care professional. Howard said he felt something give way in his spine. He managed to get off the table and leave. The chiropractor suggested he put ice on his back.

Instead, he had an emergency MRI. It turned out that Howard had three herniated discs.

The doctor told him there was a very common surgery that would offer him relief from the pain. The surgery was very straight-forward. The idea was to remove the bulging discs that were pressing on nerves that exit the spine, then fuse the bones together in those areas so they couldn't move. In theory, this meant that nothing would be rubbing against the nerves, and the pain would be gone.

It's done all the time in hospitals throughout the country. But, in Howard's case, we came to learn that it doesn't always work. In fact, it can actually make the pain worse. Anyone who has had nerve pain, even on a small scale, knows there is nothing that compares. When there is no relief from such pain, a person's quality of life is lost.

Not only did surgery fail once for Howard, but it failed a second time as well.

\* \* \*

Howard had to retire from UPS. He felt useless, he told me. He often said it was killing him to watch me go to work while he stayed home. True, he cooked better than I did – who doesn't? – but that wasn't enough to bolster his self-worth.

Toward the end of 2004, though, a new job opportunity opened up for him with the Town of Goshen Water Department. We were thrilled. Howard felt useful. He soon fell in love with the work, the slower pace and the people. The job lasted nearly two years, and we were in a good place during that time. I often stopped by for lunch and would see him laughing and joking in the break room out at the Town Garage. It was a treat for me to see him smile again. The kids sensed the change, too, and were thriving because of it.

But Howard's back pain would not move on just because he was starting to enjoy life a little, and it soon reclaimed him. I tried sending him to a physical therapist, I scheduled massage appointments for him, I got him to try acupuncture, and I sent him to counseling for depression. I could see, though, that we were losing Howard.

It was during the spring of 2006 that Howard's mental health went into a drastic decline. I got a call from him one day that spring. He had been driving a town truck and was sitting at a stop sign waiting to make a turn onto Old Route 17. From his left, heading from Chester to Goshen, a speeding car had attempted to turn onto the road where Howard was stopped. The car didn't make it. The driver slammed directly into the driver's side of the truck. Howard was broadsided by an out-of-control car. The other driver left the scene.

Basically, what would be Howard's last year of life began with a hit and run. When he called me from that truck just after he'd been slammed, I heard a voice that I barely recognized.

"I can't feel my back," he told me. The panic and desperation in his voice took my breath away. I remember him telling me many months later, after his second failed back surgery, "I should have died in that car accident."

Despite countless appointments with his surgeon and a physical therapist and months in a back brace, Howard never got better. I don't believe he ever actually sat down again. He was always either standing or lying down. He could barely drive, he couldn't sleep, he couldn't walk easily, he couldn't enjoy a moment without pain.

He was dying a slow, painful death, both physically and mentally, long before he pulled the trigger.

I have a picture of Howard holding Diesel, our golden retriever, around the time he started at the Town of Goshen Water Department. He was tall and solid in the picture, his face was bright as he held his second "son," Diesel. He looked somewhat happy.

I have another picture of him taken about eight months after his second surgery. He is a different man. There is no light in his eyes. His skin is drawn and pale, and he is very thin. He's looking at the camera but not seeing it.

When I saw that picture after Howard was dead, I cried. Why didn't I see all of that while he was alive? Why was this striking difference so evident in the picture but not in person? It looked as if his soul had slowly seeped out of him during those eight months between the pictures.

Howard disappeared during the early spring of 2007 leading up to that Memorial Day. Not in a physical sense. No, he was still in the house, still in our lives, but he was not really present.

I brought Howard to a few counselors during that time who told him he needed to address his depression even more than his back pain. Howard would always go with me. He would always agree to what was said, and he would always tell me he was taking his meds.

Yet, little by little, he was disappearing.

That March, I heard about a childhood friend who died. He had battled alcoholism his whole adult life, and rumor had it that he might have taken his own life. He'd lost his job, it was said, and he had been despondent.

I was very saddened by the news, and I told Howard about it. His reaction was alarming. He looked at me with a blank stare and then said, "Really?"

There was no shock, no sadness, no amazement – just "Really?" and he looked right past me.

I often wonder whether it was at that moment, roughly two months before Howard would take his own life, that he gave up. Did he, at that moment, decide that this was an idea worth thinking about, something to consider?

*Trish and Howard*

\*\*\*

Ironically, everyone who saw Howard at the beginning of Memorial Day weekend – on the Friday evening – noticed that he was suddenly very cheerful. He was in a great, great mood, all filled with plans. He was like a new man.

Meri O'Hara across the street told me he walked over to chat with her and Mark while they were on their front porch having a drink. He told them he was planning to take the kids camping. Craig and Scott, neighbors on each side of us, also recall brief exchanges with him that evening – the old Howard, they said.

My parents remember it as well. "Oh my God, he's doing so well," my mother said. "Like his old self!" He was smiling, laughing, talking about a trip to Florida, talking about going camping.

He had not been like this in years, and I should have seen it as a sign of something seriously wrong. It didn't register with me on a conscious level at the time, but I must have tucked it away. I don't know why people who have a suicide plan suddenly cheer up, but I'm told it's common. I'm told it's because they're so relieved that their pain is going to end soon.

The next day he didn't get out of bed. Nor the next. He was shaking, not talking except to tell me he was throwing the pills away. The pain pills. The anti-depressants. They weren't helping, he said. He stopped taking them. I begged him not to.

I didn't leave the house or take my eyes off him most of that weekend. I must have had a subconscious fear that Howard had chosen his path. I must have thought it a possibility. Hindsight again.

But by Monday afternoon, I just had to stop my vigilant watch on Howard and put the kids first for a while. I chose to spend time with my children and smile with them.

I took Luke and Trisha to the movies. I had no idea it would be the last time I'd see my husband awake … and alive.

# 5

# Paying It Forward

It was so quiet in the ER at Westchester Medical Center. This was a Level 3 trauma center and it was Memorial Day evening. Where were all the other patients? How come no one else was there? It never dawned on me then that perhaps we'd been ushered into a private area because Howard was a special case. After all, even at a Level 3 trauma center, an attempted suicide with a gunshot to the head isn't exactly your typical emergency.

So our small group stood on a private island in the middle of the ER with silence all around us –my parents and I, my brother Jimmy and my brother-in-law Richie, and Steve O'Sullivan, who had driven us down there. Not another person stood anywhere near us during those early hours there.

We had already been in the bay where Howard was lying intubated and with his head bandaged. Two doctors were in there. One had already told us there was nothing that could be done. The bullet had traveled clear across Howard's brain, he said, from the right temple to the left side of the base of his skull. He said there was no exit wound, something I already knew because I had searched for one in our bedroom when I found Howard. I don't remember doing that, actually, but I'm told I had emerged from our house with blood all over my hands. My nurse's training must have taken over for a brief moment as I moved Howard's head from left to right, looking to see if the bullet had found a way out.

That nurse in me must have kicked in again in the ER when we were officially told there was no hope, because the very first thing I said was, "Okay then. I want to donate his organs." I wonder if the doctors were a little shocked at how quickly I said that. I wonder if they were saying to themselves, "Wow, she got over that quick!" or maybe even, "Who does she have waiting in the wings and with how much money for those organs?"

I thought I should explain. I told them I'd been a nurse for twenty years and that I'd worked in the field of dialysis and renal failure for seventeen of those years. I'd watched the majority of my patients on the organ donor waiting list die without ever getting an organ.

Off the top of my head, I could name five patients of mine who were on that waiting list right in the transplant program of that very hospital where Howard was lying. Two of those five patients were young – a girl of twenty-one and a thirty-two-year-old father of three kids. They could die waiting for a kidney, and Howard was going to die no matter what. I was assured that a transplant coordinator would be in touch with me.

Organ donation was discussed again the next day when I returned to the hospital. Howard had been transferred to the ICU, where he was still intubated and gradually decompensating. He was slowly leaving us. The organ donation nurse sought me out. I told her that, without question, his two kidneys had to go to two of my patients. I essentially was making a directed donation, specifying who should get them. I wrote down the names of my dialysis patients who I knew were active on the Westchester Medical Center transplant program waiting list.

At that moment, it was critically important to me that this be done. I hoped that somehow – perhaps not for years but some day – the kids and I would be able to take some comfort knowing that Howard's organs gave others a second chance at life. Having witnessed what this second chance meant to so many of my patients, I understood the magnitude of it to those who receive such a rare gift.

The organ donation process is very fast moving, and this well oiled machine was put in place immediately. I agreed to donate Howard's kidneys, lungs, pancreas, liver, heart, corneas and skin. (No need to shudder about the skin part. They don't take it all – they just harvest it from some areas, then send it to the New York City Burn Center for use on burn victims in need of skin grafts.)

Having had four knee surgeries in my life – one involving a donated cadaver ligament – I figured I might just as well donate Howard's tendons and ligaments as well. I could see no point in his keeping them. Papers were signed. It was time to simply wait. What we were waiting for was that moment when Howard would lose all discernible brain function.

There was already a distinct difference in Howard's awareness and brain function from the time he was first seen in Arden Hill's ER, just twenty-four hours earlier. Howard was still *present* then. I know this because, when I first went to his side at Arden Hill, I bent down to whisper to him. "Was it really that bad, Howard? What was so bad? I am so sorry I didn't know." After I spoke those words, a tear ran out of Howard's left eye. It was just one solitary tear, but it was enough for me to know he heard me and understood.

And perhaps this is only the fantasy of a woman about to lose her husband, but I believe that tear was Howard's way of saying, "I am so, so sorry, Trish. But I didn't know what else to do." My own tears still come every time I allow myself to think of that moment.

The second time I knew Howard was somehow still with me happened a couple of hours later. I was alone with Howard for a brief few minutes soon after we'd been told that this was not fixable. I leaned down toward his left ear. If he was going to hear me, it would be on that side.

"It's okay, Howard," I said. I told him that, if he really wanted to go, he could. "I love you," I told him. "We all love you, and I am so sad and so sorry."

Then, for the second and last time ever in my life, I saw another solitary tear fall from the outside of Howard's left eye and roll down onto his cheek to the bottom corner of his chin. Then the tear was gone.

What I wouldn't give now to have that tear. If only I'd had a small bottle to collect it in. I have often imagined studying that tear and its makeup under a microscope. Would I have found the deep, dark sadness that plagued my husband most of his life reflected in the shape of that tear? Would I have seen a difference in, say, my tear versus his tear? What about my tears before he shot himself and those I cried after he died? Did my tears change on a cellular level?

I firmly believe they did. I believe that deep down we are all changed on a cellular level when tragedy and grief invade our lives without warning. I believe that both the kids and I have been permanently changed to our very core – from the nucleus of each cell outward. And I bet that, if someone were to research and study the tears we cry for Howard versus those we cry, say, when we injure ourselves, there would be distinct differences in the shape, makeup and color of each of those tears. That's how deep this grief has been.

But in that hospital room after Howard shed that last tear, I turned my attention elsewhere. I called my girlfriend Mary, a nurse I worked with at the dialysis unit at Good Samaritan Hospital, about twenty miles west of where Howard lay dying. I told her to tell the dialysis patients who were on Westchester's active waiting list that someone would be contacting them to come down and get tested for a possible match.

Two kidneys would soon be available.

\* \* \*

Howard remained on life support throughout Tuesday and Wednesday and was tested twice for brain function. By Tuesday evening, a full twenty-four hours after he shot himself, I sensed his spirit was very close to being separated from his broken body. His brain had gradually swollen. He was mostly gone. It got to the point where the only thing I noticed when I was with him was the sound of each machine keeping him alive. He still had corneal reflexes but they, too, were diminishing. It would not be long before, legally and medically, my husband would be declared brain dead.

By the time Trisha and Luke saw their dad to say goodbye, I don't know if his spirit was in that body or not. I like to think it was free; free but still around our children. I like to think that he was watching them from a corner of the hospital room like you read about in near-death experience stories – that he was looking down on them and seeing their anguish and then, perhaps, resting his hand on their hearts. I do know I never saw any more movement or tears, ever again.

Late that Wednesday, May 30, 2007, Howard's corneal reflexes were absent and he was declared brain dead. Doctors from the various hospital transplant programs throughout the region began preparing their patients for surgery. As I left Howard's bedside that day, I knew my own life was forever changed, and that the recipients' lives would be forever changed as well.

And I suspected that we were all crying, but for very different reasons. We were strangers connected by the death of one man. Our tears would looks so different under a microscope. I so desperately wanted my regular tears back. I didn't want these tears that seemed to come from the seat of my soul and cut like glass from my insides out.

There was no way I was going to live through this.

I visited Howard the next day. The machines were still doing their work preserving his organs, but Howard was gone. I don't even believe his spirit was in the room any longer. Howard was, I hoped, in the arms of our Lord and Savior. I said a silent prayer asking Jesus to please maybe take the kids and me as well.

On Friday morning, June 1, 2007, the Westchester transplant team took my Howard into the operating room. They disconnected the machines and tubes from his body, and they quickly took his organs and delivered them to others who had been struggling so hard to stay alive: The twenty-three-year-old man with cystic fibrosis who needed new lungs; the middle-aged diabetic who needed a new pancreas; two older adults who each needed a new cornea with which to see their grandchildren for the first time; the sixty-five-year-old gentleman from New Jersey who, I was told, had been days away from dying until he got

Howard's liver; the next fireman or toddler who would suffer severe burns and would need new skin.

And, closest to my heart, two of my dialysis patients who tested positive for a match to Howard – the thirty-two-year-old father of three who so desperately wanted to get back to work and support his family and maybe even take that long dreamed-of trip to Disney; and my sixty-three-year-old gentleman patient who was the only caretaker for his wife of forty years who had early onset Alzheimer's.

The twenty-one-year-old girl had not been a match.

All of the transplant surgeries were successful. I imagined the smiles and laughter of all of those patients and their families when they had gotten the call the night before saying, yes, they were the perfect match. By Friday afternoon they would have the organs they so desperately needed.

And then I wondered, how does it happen that we suddenly find ourselves in these places where lives are destroyed in an instant and new hope blooms at the same time for someone else? And how was I ever going to help my children find hope blooming in their own lives again?

On that Friday morning, as Howard's body lay on the operating table, and my kids slept fitfully in their own beds, and I lay crying in mine, I couldn't imagine how anything was ever going to be okay again for us. Luke, Trisha and I were now the ones who were unfixable.

No donor organ could replace what was now broken in us all – our hearts and souls.

\* \* \*

It would be sooner than I had hoped, though, that I was able to take some measure of peace – and even laughter – from giving Howard's organs away.

The thirty-two-year-old father of three kids who received one of Howard's kidneys had not been told at first how this kidney had become available. The staff members at the Good Sam dialysis unit were careful not to discuss my family tragedy, particularly during those early days while Howard was still technically alive.

He had no way of knowing who might have died when he was brought to Westchester to have his blood tested for a possible match. When it turned out that he was nearly an exact match, he was called and told to get back to the hospital for surgery the next day. He was also told that he was receiving a directed donation – someone had specified that he was to be the recipient. No one told him that the kidney belonged to the brain-dead husband of the nurse manager at his dialysis unit.

The patient was taken totally off guard when he was told it was a directed donation. "By whom?" he asked. He knew of no one willing to give him a kidney. The surgeon told him he didn't know where it came from but that this kidney was specifically donated to him.

Eventually, after he'd had his surgery and was on the mend, he called my co-worker Mary and asked her who had donated this kidney to him. Mary said she would need to get permission from the person involved – that would be me – before telling him. I said yes, she could have him call me and I would gladly tell him the entire story.

I got a call the next day from this very teary but ecstatic former patient. "Trish," he said, "I cannot believe you donated a kidney to me!" He was blubbering his thanks, and I quickly realized that he thought I had donated one of *my* kidneys to him. That brought a smile to my face.

I explained that, no, even though I was very fond of him, I didn't actually give him a kidney of my own. I said that, in fact, I have two sisters with kidney issues, so my kidneys were already spoken for should the need arise.

Then I had to tell him the story of Howard. As would happen countless times in the coming weeks and months, I found myself reassuring someone else that it was okay, we would be okay and that I was so happy for him. I assured him that, in fact, donating Howard's organs was a blessing for me.

Did I believe any of that at that time? No, not a bit. I didn't think we would be okay, this wasn't okay, and I still didn't perceive it as a blessing. As a matter of fact, it was what was going to kill us, I was sure.

It would be long years before I gained faith that we'd all survive. But it was only a few short days later that my brother Jimmy helped us begin to laugh about the organ donation when he spoke about it at Howard's funeral.

"The people who received Howard's organs will be shocked at how athletic they might become," he said. "They shouldn't be surprised to discover that, all of a sudden, they can throw a ninety-mile-per-hour fast ball."

# 6

# Saying Goodbye

During the four days Howard was on life support, people kept asking me if he was going to make it. Some even told me they were praying that he'd live. I said thanks but no thanks.

"I sure hope doesn't make it," I told these people who meant so well with their prayers. "Because if he does, he'll be a vegetable."

I didn't want that, and he obviously didn't either. When Howard pulled the trigger, his goal sure wasn't to lie in a nursing home bed for the next few years.

The kids and I said goodbye that Thursday, May 31, 2007. I brought them in and had them each spend some time alone with him. Their time with him was very brief – how could it not be? What do a twelve-year-old and a fourteen-year-old know about saying goodbye to their dad after he shoots himself?

I don't remember what I said to him either, not in its entirety. I do know I prayed, and I asked Howard to forgive me for all that I did wrong as a wife and for not knowing how to stop him. And I told him it was okay to leave – to really leave this earth. I know I asked him to please, please look out for the three of us as it was going to take a miracle to get us through this.

As I write this, I wonder what I could have been thinking half the time while Howard was lying down there in a coma. I know I kept doing things – I went to bed, got up, talked to people, pretended to myself that I had it all under control and that all those around me believed I was on top of things.

I kept it up after he was officially dead, too. In retrospect, I can't believe I actually drove downtown alone to Donovan's Funeral Home to pick out my dead husband's casket. Oh yeah, right. I had it all under control. For crying out loud, I shouldn't have even been allowed to drive a car let alone go decide about coffins by myself. White, brown, waterproof, bug proof? Who knew? I ended up getting a somewhat ornate brown coffin that I believe had an extra layer or two of padding – I think. I don't remember, exactly, and I can't go check.

But I didn't crash the car on the way down there or back. A miracle, really.

I think I was doing a little hysterical laughing around that time, too. One thing that struck me extremely funny at the time happened while everyone in the family was looking through my boxes of pictures to display during Howie's wake. Naturally, given my penchant for disarray, they were saved in large plastic bins that most people use for storing clothes, and they were completely disorganized.

My brothers, sisters, parents, in-laws, nieces and nephews – everyone had a bin, a stack or a handful of pictures. After about an hour, my daughter Trisha came to me with one picture in her hand and a horrified look on her face. I thought it must be a picture of her dad, possibly taken at a very tender moment.

She closely guarded the picture so that no one else could see what she was showing me. She slowly turned it over so I could see it, and as I stood with her staring at it, she said, "WHO is this and why do you have it?" I cannot adequately describe the horror and shock on my daughter's face.

So what did I do? I burst out laughing. The picture was of Beverly, one of my girlfriends, taken during our trip to Cancun about four years earlier. It was pouring rain and, without doubt, there were only four people in the Caribbean Sea that day – my four girlfriends, all quite drunk and happily swimming in the sea quite, quite naked.

I was the person on shore holding the camera, and the shot I caught was something to behold. In it, Beverly had just dutifully obeyed a command from Peggy: "On three, everyone jump up with your arms in the air!"

And there, caught on film, was Beverly – the one in our group with the largest boobs – completely out of the water from her waist up, her size DD breasts exposed for all the world to see. And I think all the world actually did see.

Right after taking that picture, I heard a cacophony of clicking cameras behind me. I turned to look back at our seven-story hotel. It appeared that all of the hotel guests were standing on their balconies filming my four friends in the sea, one of whom took very seriously the command to "jump up on three." I suspect Beverly has a special place in several of their holiday photo albums.

Despite our grim task, I just had to laugh at the memory when Trisha showed me that picture.

\* \* \*

I had to get my kids some clothes for their father's wake and funeral. Luke, who was finishing eighth grade, had grown at least four inches the previous year. Of course he owned no dress clothes that fit – no dress shoes, shirt, pants, belt, tie – not even socks.

I hadn't a clue what size dress Trisha might need. She was in the midst of her tomboy stage, and she pretty much only wore her brother's shorts and shirts.

Off to Kohl's I went, along with the two kids and my brother Jimmy's credit card. This was on Saturday, before the first wake. I was running on adrenaline. I hadn't eaten or drunk anything in days as far as I remember.

The only thing I recall about that shopping trip was standing on the line to pay for the kids' new clothes. It was there that it hit me like a ton of bricks had been thrown at my chest. "My God! Howard killed himself, and here I am with the kids getting clothes for his funeral! How the hell did this happen?"

I was physically sick and couldn't risk standing there any longer. I pulled the kids off the line and took them and the new clothes over to the ladies room. They dutifully waited outside the bathroom while I went into the bathroom and threw up.

I wondered if I was going insane. I felt like taking the last step into a breakdown. I was in a state of utter terror – and in Kohl's of all places.

I wanted to run. I recall leaving the bathroom and finding myself standing next to the kids outside the bathroom door. I stood there hesitating for a few moments, not really knowing how to get out of the building. But a little voice in the back of my brain kept telling me I had to function long enough to get back on line and give the cashier my brother's credit card.

I don't know what the kids thought. The three of us were so very numb that I don't know whether they even noticed that their mom was standing there frozen and staring. We must have gotten out of the store at some point because we're not still standing there, a tableau of three people frozen in time outside the Kohl's bathroom.

And I must have paid because I wasn't arrested for shoplifting. I don't recall how we got out of there, though.

\* \* \*

Two nights before Howard's wake, I woke up at around 4 a.m. I had an overwhelming need to write a note to someone – I don't know who, specifically, but I wanted to ask someone, everyone, to please come to the wake and to please forgive Howard and to remember him and us.

I got up, sat at the computer and just started typing. The words flowed out of me effortlessly, from where I have no idea. Maybe divine intervention? Certainly, in the shape I was in, there wasn't a chance I could have written a shopping list on my own let alone a three-page letter I'd just produced for those who would be at the wake.

I put a picture of Howard on it – one that captured him in a good place. You can see it in his smile and his eyes. I also put a Bible verse on it that the kids helped me choose.

That letter appears here, at the end of this chapter.

I took the letter to Linda's Office Supply downtown and asked her to please make copies for me to hand out at the wake. I didn't know how many. Linda just went ahead and made one thousand copies of that three-page letter. She suspected we would need them. And she was right. We needed them.

A lot of people came to the wakes that Sunday and Monday. A lot. Some of my friends and neighbors told me they waited forty-five minutes or more to get into the building. The line wound its way through two rooms in Donovan's Funeral Home, out the front door and down South Church Street.

I ran out of the letters during the first wake, and Linda made more for the second. She doesn't tell anyone that she did it all for free.

Where did all these people come from, the thousand plus people who streamed through Donovan's for Howard Nelson's wake? For the wake of a man who killed himself? To see him laid out down at Donovan's?

Well, family to start with. And friends, too. Howard and I had been in Goshen more than twenty-three years. You get to know a lot of people in twenty-three years.

The kids knew a lot of people, too; far more than they actually realized: Boy Scouts, Girl Scouts, school teams, travel baseball, dance school, trumpet lessons, church groups, play dates, and all the town events that make up a young family's life – parades, fairs, farmers markets, firehouse events, holidays, friends' parties and celebrations.

They all came. The kids' friends and ours. My neighbors. My parents' neighbors in Surrey Meadows. The scouts. The sports teams. The volunteer fire fighters. Howard's childhood friends and mine. His oldest daughters, Tara, Selina and Heather. His co-workers from UPS and the village water department. My siblings' friends. My brother Jimmy's battalion from the New York City Fire Department. My parents' friends. School teachers. Even the kids' pre-school teachers. My co-workers at Good Samaritan. My mother's co-workers from Social Services. People from the local churches who barely knew us.

I remember only small moments. I don't remember seeing many of those who came. I was present but detached. I stood through it all. I shook hands, kissed cheeks, received kisses, hugged hundreds and cried with a few, but not many.

I remember I developed a rash on my face from all the facial hair I was rubbing up against with each kiss. I remember that some people thought my sister Ann was a nun because, as each person came by, I said, "This is my sister Ann." We decided I should change how I introduced her. And yes, we laughed.

I remember Luke's friend Marlee, the fourteen-year-old daughter of funeral director Mark Johnston, helping out at the wakes. She later wrote Luke a beautiful letter. We still have it.

I remember hearing soft voices of people who were wondering aloud about how Howard killed himself. Did he shoot himself? Where's the bullet hole? We had an open casket and there was no visible evidence that Howard had shot himself in the temple. He looked just like Howard, only thinner.

Looking at my husband in the casket, a large part of me could simply not comprehend that he was dead, never to wake up. Maybe it was my mind's way of not allowing it all in at once so that the full knowledge wouldn't kill me.

\* \* \*

I also clearly remember one of the actual funny things that happened while Howard was laid out in his coffin down at Donovan's.

It was toward the end of the wake, and it was time to close up Howard's coffin. Trisha had placed her favorite stuffed animal into the coffin next to her father's head – an orange cat she'd named Howie years earlier when she'd gotten it at Build-A-Bear. The cat was wearing a fireman outfit, complete with black boots.

When it came time to close the coffin lid, Howie the cat was removed and returned to her. But one of the cat's black boots had come off and was still in the coffin with Howard.

"His shoe!" Trisha wailed. "I need Howie's shoe!"

Easily fixed, of course, except that my brother-in-law Richie thought it was *Howard's* shoe that Trisha wanted.

"Oh shit," he said as he headed toward the closed coffin. "Am I going to have to crawl in there and yank off one of Howard's shoes for her?!"

He would have done it, too, but I stopped him.

"No, no, it's the cat's shoe she wants," I told him. "Just find the cat's shoe up near the top of Howard."

Richie was greatly relieved. So was Trisha when she got Howie the cat's small black boot back.

\* \* \*

The morning of the funeral was a blur. Who got dressed with whose help? I don't know. I couldn't breathe on the drive to the funeral home. I felt like a vise had been placed around my torso and was slowly tightening.

The funeral home – all those tears, all those eyes with no sparkle left. And then the slide show of photos my brother Johnny had put together – I felt I would break into a million pieces. The sadness took on a life of its own. I had no energy nor will to fight it. I let it have its way with me.

It was my turn up at the casket. I looked at Howard's face and wondered if there was a way to burn his image into my mind. My soul. What struck me so deeply was that right then, right in that room, I was gazing upon my husband's face for the very last time. I just couldn't wrap my mind around that.

I figured I had two choices. I could stay rooted to the spot and look at him forever, perhaps succumbing to hysteria at some point. Or I could say goodbye. I could look upon Howard for the last time, and stand up and say, okay, it's time to put the lid down.

I chose the latter. I said goodbye and told Howard I would see him in heaven. Then I turned my back on the casket and walked among the living.

The bagpipes played.

The casket was closed after we left. I imagine Howard looking up at Mark as he closed it for the final time. I have often wondered what Mark thinks when he puts his hand on the coffin lid and is the last person to see the dead.

\* \* \*

The limousines took the kids and my parents and me away from the funeral. We were headed towards the cemetery but first the firemen had planned a goodbye and brief prayer for Howard at the Minisink Hook and Ladder Company on North Church Street.

There were a lot of people mad at Howard for killing himself, especially his fellow firefighters. Some of them, I think, still are. I probably didn't fully realize it at the time, but these firefighters and my friends and family were so very angry that he could have done such a thing to me and to the kids. And to himself.

Still, they were there for us, there for Howard. And it was something to see. The firemen – you know how they do a funeral. It was massive, with fire trucks and a long line of cars and a huge flag hung down in the center of North Church Street, right in front of the firehouse where Howard had spent so many happy hours.

Our limousine pulled up, and the kids and I got out. There, by the flag pole, the firemen said their goodbyes. The men all around me were crying. They gave me an American flag in Howard's honor.

There was only one last thing to do for Howard, and that was to put him in the ground. We got back into the cars and turned around, heading back past Donovan's out South Church Street to the old Slate Hill Cemetery at the edge of town. Some of the tombstones there are overgrown with moss they've been there so long.

A lot of people went. I remember being lifted by that – most people don't usually go to the cemetery. Some people stood close by, some off on their own up on the hills, the grass, or the dirt road that weaves through the headstones.

I stood at the top portion of the hole in the ground with Howard's casket hovering over it and draped in flowers. I remember my parents standing directly behind me. I still can hear my mother softly crying. The only words I remember hearing as I stood there are the ones my father spoke into my ear when he broke down sobbing: "Trish, what are you going to do?"

And I lied. "Dad, it is going to be okay," I told him.

Then it was over. We left Howard there to be put in the ground after we were gone. He'd be keeping company with folks who'd been buried there for more than two hundred years. I suppose that, two hundred years from now, people will marvel at the overgrown moss on his tombstone, too.

Luke, Trisha and I went back to our house on Oxford Road. And there, in the weeks and months and years to come, the three of us gradually disappeared, too.

For a long, long time.

The following was handed out to all who went to the wake.

*Howard John Nelson*

*To My Howard:*

*You are my husband, lover, best friend and soul mate. I will keep you alive with us every day while we are apart.*
*I cannot wait to get one of your "pick me up off the ground" bear hugs when we meet in heaven. Please be the first to answer the door when I arrive.*
*I will love you forever,*

*Your Wife (or as you would say to me, "my cute little darling")*

*".... And be sure of this: I am with you always, even to the end of the age." – Matthew 28:20*

With great sadness, we say goodbye to a husband, father, brother, son-in-law, brother-in-law, best friend, co-worker, neighbor and the best all-around greatest guy one could ever have had the pleasure of knowing. And of course, in my opinion, the most handsome, sexy man to ever have lived.

Howard touched so many lives – more than he ever could know. He had an effect on each person he met, and he never even knew it. Howard's suffering and anguish these past few years was not who he was and should not overshadow the beautiful times we have all shared with him and the blessings he has brought into each of our lives.

Howard loved me with all his heart, and I loved him fiercely. I think back to our first times together, and my heart laughs and skips a few beats remembering his romantic side and love letters. Just as with all marriages, finding our way during the early years was so awkward, so much fun and so new and promising. Then came Luke and then Trisha right on his heels, and life made a full 360-degree turn – but still we had so many laughs, milestones and, above all else, so much hope, just as all young families have.

It cannot be said often enough that each day does matter. Howard packed all he could into each moment he was walking this earth. He was a phenomenal athlete as those of you who had to bat against him when he was a pitcher can attest to. I've heard hundreds of times that he was the best softball player in the county. How I loved watching his 6'3" frame run so effortlessly across center field to catch a long fly ball.

Howard was a great outdoorsman and spent much of his free time outside. I would often have to go looking for him well after dark to see if he was ever coming in. He told me once that he remembered being only six years old and wanting nothing more than to be in the woods. He thought heaven was being up at Mark's hunting cabin with Richie and the crew for a week out in the cold woods. (I guess it's a man thing.)

We all know Howard's love for kids – his gentle teasing and fun games with his nieces and nephews. All of them have awesome memories of Uncle Howard to carry with them through life. He was downright belly laughter funny with them, as his *Wizard of Oz* Tin Man picture can attest to. His love for Luke and Trisha was so powerful and endless that at times I thought he could never sustain that intensity. His love and pride for his older daughters – Tara, Selina and Heather (his girls, as he called them) – was just as strong. I can say to them with no hesitation that he felt so blessed and amazed to have such beautiful daughters.

Howard loved nothing more than to teach Luke and Trisha the fine art of baseball and softball and he relished being able to teach their friends to play as well. He possessed such patience when teaching young boys how to field a grounder and hit a ball correctly. "These guys have to learn the basics first," was a common pronouncement in our house.

And who could forget how much fun he poked at the Kitson family – how he teased us all? Until just last week, he always found a way to joke about us, about how much we all talked at the same time and never left each other alone. All the while, he would have this little grin on his face and he'd follow his teasing with a quick peck on the cheek, telling me he loved us all. And he did – my family embraced Howard into the flock more than twenty-three years ago, and we have never let go of him.

Howard's childhood friends – we don't ever realize while we are kids just what an impact those friendships have on us later in life. Howard's childhood friends were his lifeline during his teen years, and to this day they remain a part of his heart that no one else had access to.

I would be remiss if I didn't mention Howard's devotion and strong love for the many canines in his life – Doki, Chili, Diesel and Daisy. All I can say is that it was magical watching him with our dogs and seeing their reaction to his love for them.

The UPS guys, the Town of Goshen Water Department guys, the A+ Sewer guys (or, as Trisha would say, the Pooper Scoopers) – Howard shined when he was with you fellows. He laughed, he joked, he lived life to the fullest when working with all of you. You will never know what working with men such as all of you meant to Howard, but I know – I know it meant life to him. I saw it in him every day, and then I saw that life seep out of him when he could no longer work. Watching that joy in him die was almost as sad for me as losing him now. Howard's days with you were so much funnier than mine, and you will forever remind me of Howard. What an amazing blessing.

Howard absolutely loved being the best friend and neighbor anyone could have. He needed to be that way and it filled his life with such happiness to do for others, even if it simply meant fixing their lawn mower. He never asked for anything, and he never expected anything. For Howard, the joy was in the doing.

And finally, the Grace Community Baptist Church and the Minisink Hook and Ladder Fire Company – all I can say is that both these organizations and their members came along at times in Howard's life when he needed them most. You saved his life and his soul during those times, and I am blessed because of all of you.

God brings people into our lives to bless us during our most difficult and tragic times. Our blessings have come in the form of Howard, and now that Howard has gone on to be with Jesus, in the form of all of you. We want to thank you all for your support, love, kindness, compassion and, best of all, your love for our Howard.

Celebrate Howard's life each day – remember when he helped you, laughed with you, embraced you, worked with you, or just simply talked with you. By keeping him daily in your conversations, thoughts and hearts, you help us live on and help keep Howard alive for all of us.

# 7

# Under the Microscope

My life as it had been was over. Gone. I was still a mother, sister, daughter, friend, neighbor, registered nurse, dog lover, but now there was a new word added to that list – widow. And that added title loomed over everything else. There was the word *WIDOW* above me now, forming an arc over the kids, the dogs and me.

We were the family with no husband or father. Not only had there been a death in the family, but there had been a *suicide*. That word added so much more of a burden. The change this brought about in the dynamic of our family relationships with one another – that alone was monumental. I can't overstate just how dramatic and shattering this shift was. The very way we acted and responded to each other as an intact unit was now completely wiped away. It was as if a custodian had come along with an eraser and wiped the chalk board clean.

There we were, the three of us, with a clean slate staring us in the face. We would have to write a new family unit on that blank slate. Over time, we would find that our actions and reactions, our bad choices and good ones would all play a role in filling up that slate. But that big blank – there was nothing as frightening as that emptiness.

In the beginning, we pulled together instinctively. We surrounded each other and offered support to the weakest member at that moment. And we all took on the role of weakest member, although Mommy not so much. How could I? There were two young teenagers in the house who needed a free pass to be the weakest, most vulnerable and neediest in the group. There was no time in the beginning for Mommy to even acknowledge her devastation, insecurity and absolute terror.

This pulling together extended out the front door to our family, friends, neighbors and even casual acquaintances. They took turns as forces surrounding us, protecting us and providing for us. It was as it should be during a tragedy – people entered our lives to give us so many of our daily necessities, bringing food, walking the dogs, giving the kids rides to and from wherever, listening and comforting when the house was dark and lonely.

But all of this love and support, this protection and security meant the loss of one basic human need – privacy. Our lives were now under scrutiny from my family and friends who judged every nuance in my tone of voice; from the neighbors who watched us come and go and turn lights on and off; from the merchants down town to the teachers at the kids' school. Everyone was watching us like hawks.

Think about it. Every action I took as a newly widowed mom was observed, noted, debated and commented upon. There was no getting around it. If I was going to allow people to help us, I also had to be willing to give up my privacy.

I think of a family I heard of about a year and a half after Howard died. A mom with three kids. The father had also killed himself. They were of Asian background and much more private than our loud, close-knit Irish family. I remember hearing about the mom who, just one week after the suicide of her husband, began isolating herself from her church acquaintances and her friends.

She sent people away from her door when they brought over food. They should donate it to the food pantry, she told them. She attended church but refused the visits of other parishioners and their offers to help clean, organize and assist any way they could. She assured everyone that she really had it together and that she and the kids wanted privacy as they embarked on their journey of grief.

I was amazed by her. Could I – or did I even had the right to – choose privacy over help? I didn't even know what I was doing from one minute to the next. I was in no shape to reject any offer of help.

Actually, I could barely function. Yes, the kids got fed. Yes, I cleaned, did laundry, drove the kids to where they were supposed to be. I met with Social Security, I walked the dogs and, weirdly enough, just three weeks after Howie died, I took Luke and Trisha on the family vacation to the Florida Keys that we had planned with him.

I did pretty well on the day to day stuff. But to allow no one else into our world to help? I don't think it even occurred to me that I could choose that.

Remember when Hillary Clinton said, "It takes a village to raise a child"? Well, as I think back on those early days, I realize it took a village to get the three of us to a place where we could function independently. I needed the support, the wisdom, the prayers and love we got by allowing our lives to be an open book. But we were so exposed to our village! Everyone was maintaining a vigilant watch to make sure the three of us weren't going off the deep end.

I have to laugh now thinking about my siblings and parents looking at the three of us at a family gathering soon after Howard killed himself: Me staring off into the middle distance; Luke sitting mute but with a smile pasted on his face; and Trisha with this very dark piece of hair – she dyed only the front piece of her blond hair – covering one eye so no one could see her face.

How many of them had to be wondering, "What the hell are we going to do with them?"

I laugh because we are all so helpless at times, aren't we, even as we pretend we're just fine, thank you? Even though I was telling myself we had it all under control, we were really such a mess and we weren't fooling anyone. The three of us were like an exposed tooth nerve. Just breathing in and out hit us like cold air hitting that raw nerve.

So many people saw me at my worst. (Well, almost – I saved the worst of the worst for me alone). Still, I cringe now when I think of all the people who saw me at my neediest, most devastated, most out of control. Damn, that's hard to swallow. Where was my dignity, for crying out loud?!

I often asked those around me, "How am I doing? ... What should I do about this? ... Is what I'm doing here sound and sane?" I asked both my brother Jimmy and sister-in-law Diane to keep tabs on how I was acting. I wanted to know how I was functioning from their point of view, and I needed them to let me know if I was veering off track. A little off track was okay – I was a little off track for a long, long time – but I needed their input if I was making dangerous and destructive decisions, especially in terms of Trisha and Luke. I wanted to be one hundred percent right with the kids.

If I wasn't, I was sure they'd turn out insane.

I imagine all parents question decisions they make affecting their kids. That's normal, and it's a good idea to re-examine what kind of parents we are once in a while. But throw a suicide into the mix and my re-examining was paralyzing. I couldn't even decide whether pizza for dinner was appropriate. As it happens, we had pizza most nights the first two years after the suicide. I should own Goshen Village Pizza by now.

I wonder now, what did everyone think of me during those first few weeks? Months? What did they think when they saw me frantically walking miles through the Village of Goshen? Most nights, I swear I was walking a nine-minute mile – faster than some runners. I had that iPod on, blasting songs into my head as I moved my legs as fast as I could.

I have always been a runner (or walker, depending on my conditioning), and Goshen was where I had run for the previous twenty-one years. But now I imagined everyone staring at me. What were they thinking? Did people look at me and wonder, "My God, how is she coping?" Or, "How can she be out walking after what happened?" Or, "Has she lost her mind?" Or maybe, in my wildest hopes, "Wow, she has great legs!"

For the first two years, people came into our house without even knocking. My every move was scrutinized by those who loved me ... and several who didn't.

"Why is she doing that?"
"She shouldn't do that."
"She should just do that."
"Those kids need this."
"She's spending too much money."
"She needs to get back to work."
"She cannot stay in that house."
"She cannot leave that house."
"I don't think she should be dating."
"I think she should be dating."
"Doesn't she know she isn't the only one who has lost someone?"
"She should think about others now."
"She should go to church more."
"She should leave it all in God's hands."
"She should take control of everything."
"It's all about the kids now."
"She shouldn't let the kids get away with so much."
"She shouldn't make the kids do anything."

So there I was, allowing others to help me make decisions and navigate through the haze of our grief and our everyday lives. I felt watched and a little pummeled, but I think the kids felt it much more intensely, especially in school. They both began keeping to themselves.

Did anyone really have any idea how much we suffered? And how some days just getting up was a triumph? There are those in my life who knew full well what we endured. They were the ones who, day in and day out, stood watch over us. I will be forever grateful to them.

It would be three and a half years before Luke, Trisha and I began to reclaim some of our privacy. I remember the three of us deciding together that it was time to close the curtains a little bit. We decided to discuss things as a family first, and that we wouldn't pull others in to help until we all agreed to do so.

That was our turning point. It was when we became an actual family of three. The kids knew they could trust me, and I began to trust myself. It took courage to tell those who had stood guard over us for all those years that it was time to back off now. It was hard for me to say, "No, it's okay. I've got this one." And it was hard for those who had heaped their love and support on us to step back and let us make our own way. It must have felt like rejection, like a bit of an insult.

But, like I said, it was nearly four years before we were standing on our own without wobbling ... and falling ... and throwing ourselves to the ground. And believe me when I tell you, there were times I didn't think any of us would get out of our grief alive.

# 8

# Heading for a Breakdown

I went on leave from my job at Good Sam's dialysis unit immediately after burying Howard. Three months later, I resigned.

I had to. The kids needed me at home. The school year was about to end and, at twelve and fourteen, Luke and Trisha were too old for a babysitter but too young and traumatized to sit at home alone with their grief. There was some insurance money and savings to tide me over for a while. Not forever, but for a while.

Filling my idle time was really a no-brainer. First, I had to figure out how to get rid of Howard's belongings – his clothes, his truck, his guns. I discovered early on that getting rid of his internal organs was a whole lot easier than getting rid of his shirts and underwear. Almost immediately, I was paralyzed. I couldn't do it. Howard's pick-up truck sat in the driveway for months, blocking my own way in and out half the time. His clothes ate up my closet space. Howard was everywhere in the house and, for a long time, I simply let him stay.

In part, I was paralyzed by fear. I learned early on that fear was to be my constant companion. I literally spent three years being scared. I tried hard to control it, but I could not. The worst of my fears was that one of the kids would also become a suicide

– this was to become a very real possibility, as it turned out, and I knew it would be the end of my own life, too.

    I feared this constantly for the first three years after Howard died. I could not comfortably bring myself to leave them alone in the house for those entire three years. I would endlessly check in even if I went no farther than the grocery store. I'd text, I'd call, I'd rush home from wherever I went. I was always afraid of what I'd find when I opened the front door.

    Most often, the worst case scenario does not happen in life, but it had happened in mine. I lived with the knowledge that bad things, uncontrollable things, do happen. The fear ate me alive and apparently ate my stomach up as well. I ended up with several ulcers. Living with such fear also eats up a lot of energy, both mental and physical, and I often felt exhausted.

    Despite my profound exhaustion, I spent those first six months in movement. Constant movement. Everything I did became a physical feat. Some of it involved gardening or, more accurately, ripping out bushes, dirt and rocks by hand. Instead of merely cleaning the house, I began hauling pieces of furniture from one room to another. I vacuumed the pool until there was not one tiny piece of foreign matter in it. I was determined to take over all the household maintenance, both inside and out. I wanted to *own* this responsibility even if it killed me.

    And I continued exercising. I walked miles and miles, sometimes alone, sometimes with the dogs. I started lifting kettle bells for hours at a time, until I could push press sixty-three pounds over my head with one arm. I worked out on the elliptical, I peddled the exercise bike on an endless road to nowhere, I worked out at boot camp.

    And all the while, whether I was walking or gardening or lifting kettle bells, I had music blasting in my ears. Oddly enough, I was choosing music that Howard hadn't liked – Guns N Roses, Bon Jovi, Elton John, Matchbox 20, Santana. It was weird.

    I must have seemed like a maniac. I think it actually was a grief-induced mania. I guess it could have been worse. I could have been down at the bar or hitting the bottle of Xanax and Percocets daily. But I wasn't. Actually I didn't have a drink of alcohol for eighteen months after Howard died. I didn't want to go there, and it was probably one of the sanest decisions I made during that period of my life. The last thing I needed was the depressing effects of alcohol. I was depressed enough as it was, thank you very much.

Was it just the grief that propelled me madly forward almost as soon as the funeral was over? No doubt that was a big part of it. But it was determination that I wasn't going to let this defeat me. On one hand, I felt beaten already. Something else had won my husband. But I wasn't going to let it get anymore of me or my children.

And I didn't know how to stop. It didn't even register with me that I could not keep this pace up forever. I went on like this until, almost exactly six months later, I crashed.

\* \* \*

It was on my way home from the first Worker's Compensation hearing that I finally lost it. I finally crumbled into a heap of pain and weeping.

It was six months after Howard died, and I'd just faced a miserable creep at that hearing, where people seemed determined to make my life harder than it already was. There was an insurance adjuster there who was absolutely horrid. The guy made an arrogant comment about Howard's suicide.

If I'd had the energy, I would have reached across the table and beaten the shit out of his squashy, fat face. I could have done it, too. I had been lifting kettlebells for about six months by that point.

Anyway, I was driving home and it just let loose. Just as I turned onto Route 17K in Newburgh, six months' worth of pain and despair just welled up from the depth of my being. I began sobbing. And sobbing. Oh my God, it was deadly.

Somehow, I pulled off the road. I wanted to disappear – no, actually, I wanted to die. It is one of few times since Howard shot himself that I truly wanted to die. The pain was so horrible, so relentless, so foreign and so very, very deep that I wanted out.

I cried for weeks after that. It lasted all through the holidays. I just cried my way through Thanksgiving and Christmas and New Years. It's basically all I did.

I was still mainly just crying in early January and, for some reason, I chose that particular moment in time to have the total knee replacement that I'd been needing for years. Why? Who knows? Why not?

And, of course, that didn't improve my state of mind. After the surgery, I was forced to be idle. Finally and suddenly idle. I couldn't pull bushes out of the ground or haul furniture around or clean the house or walk the dogs or run and run and run. I couldn't run away from my anguish.

Instead, I had to lie in bed and think. And cry. And wallow in the pain.

And finally, one day, it stopped. I was done, at least with the wallowing. My tear ducts dried up, my knee surgery healed, I got out of my bed and picked up the reins of my life and started lugging my grief around with me with again.

*  *  *

Everyone deals with grief differently – there are thousands of books out there that tell you so.

In my case, I thought of my grief as a large suitcase that I had to bring with me wherever I went. It came along to the store, the gym, the doctor's office, into the elevator, to work, to my friend's house, to the restaurant. I carried it when I went to see family, I took it outside while I cleaned the pool and mowed the lawn, I brought it into the shower and into bed. I could not leave it behind no matter how hard I tried, no matter how many bushes I pulled from the yard or how many miles I walked. It was there whether I was sleeping or awake.

It was HUGE at the beginning, and I couldn't even tell you what was in that suitcase. I just knew it was mine to deal with. I don't know how one's physical body deals with such a burden. There were times I thought for sure this heavy weight attached to me would cause me to crumble and turn to dust as I sat there.

What I finally realized was that, although I had been carrying my grief around with me, I really hadn't allowed myself to start grieving, to actually experience my pain until that day I fell apart in the car on 17K. My mind had initiated a cascade of self-protective systems that allowed only so much to enter my world; otherwise I would die.

That's true of everyone. We all need self-protection for a while – maybe for weeks or months, maybe even for years. We want nothing more than to get away from the pain – as far away as possible. We can't face the full force of it.

In my case, I had been running for cover, and I had started running the day I went down to Donovan's Funeral Home to pick out a casket for my dead husband. As I got out of my car that day and started up the sidewalk to the funeral home to meet with Mark, the following words began to echo inside my head:

*You better run for cover!*

I heard the words in my head and may even have said them out loud. My God, I wanted to run. I stood on that sidewalk and I remember having the conscious realization, right then and there, that the rest of my life was going to be bad. Real bad. I didn't want to walk into that funeral home. I wanted to run.

\* \* \*

Running for cover was the most attractive thought in my life for a long time. I wanted out – I didn't want to have to do this grief thing and didn't want to have to do life with this suicide thing. I didn't want to raise two kids alone, let alone two kids whose father had killed himself. Having to do life and my kids lives in the shadow of it was more than I thought I could ever handle. And I didn't want to. There had to be a way out – there had to be somewhere to hide.

Sometimes, to this day, I still wish it away. Especially on those days Trisha is having a hard time, or Luke seems distant, or I am overcome with feelings of fear of another loss or disappointment. They say you can take these tragic life events and use them to grow, become a more evolved human being, a better version of yourself. Fine, great, whatever. I still wish it away, pretty sure that I would have been okay with that other version of myself, the pre-suicide version, and didn't need this as a self-improvement plan.

And sometimes, I still feel occasional bitterness at Howard for doing this to me, to us. Yes, intellectually I get it – he was in pain, he was depressed, he was a wounded soul who could take no more – but damn it all anyway!

I will say this for grief, though. If you embrace it and face it, it eventually forces you to start living life one day at a time. Most of us don't live in the moment. We are told we should, but how many of us can do that? We are told to not answer the door when our past knocks, as it has nothing new to say. We are told not to live for the future, that all we have right now is the present. But living life that way is difficult.

But this debilitating grief forced me to begin living in the moment. Not in that good way, the way people advise you to take all you can from each moment, to live, laugh, love! No, for the grief-stricken, the moment is the only safe place. I didn't dare stay too long in the past. I could not, or I'd have gone insane. I didn't dare dream of the future. I had already seen the other shoe drop and I knew it could easily happen again. I had no idea how I was even going to *make* it to the future. I could barely breathe – how the hell was I going to make it to tomorrow, through lunch tomorrow or through after school and dinner tomorrow? I was simply on autopilot.

And then I stopped. It took at least a year, but I stopped running for cover. Was it the prayers of others and the hand of God on us? Was it that I was really as strong as people told me? Was it something deep inside that propelled me forward towards healing and re-entering the land of the living?

I don't know. But at some point, I stopped carrying that suitcase around and invited grief in. I understood that I had to embrace the grief in order to get through it to the other side. After all, if I didn't start, I wasn't ever going to get to stop.

And so I began charting my way.

# 9

# Grief Journal
## The First Year

*September 2007*

I came into the house calling out Howard's name. I realized a few days after that – after the day he killed himself – that I'd gotten into the habit of calling out Howard's name each time I entered the house.

I opened the door and called out his name all at the same time. As soon as I stepped in, I saw both Diesel and Daisy looking at me from downstairs. They had been put down there by Howard, and the child gate was closed and locked. They were wagging their tails, very happy to see us.

Howard did not answer my call, and I started up the stairs. As I did, I noticed a loud snoring sound. I don't remember if the bedroom door was closed or not, but the sound grew louder as I walked closer. I was thinking of how Howard snored when he was tired.

I entered the bedroom and saw him on the floor, lying on his back. Blood was coming out of his nose and mouth. His hands were at his side, covered in blood. I remember yelling, "What happened here? Did you fall? I don't get this!" I remember saying all those things a few times.

I remember looking at Howard's head, and I think I tried to find an exit wound. Very weird how this was all going on in a matter of seconds, but remembering it now, it feels like it took a lifetime to happen.

I remember the gun lying in the middle of the bed, and I remember thinking, how could he be lying flat on the floor if the gun is in the middle of the bed? Why do his hands have blood on them? Did he grab his head after he shot himself? Did he fall and hit his head on the dog crate? I remember saying several times, "I don't get this, Howard!" I also remember looking for a note – I looked for a note on the bed, but I didn't see one.

I wonder now, did Howard hear me? Did he know I was there? Could he see me looking at him and did he hear me ask all those questions? Does he now understand what it did to me to find him like that? With half his head blown off and him lying there seizing?

I cannot believe my body didn't fall apart during those first seconds as I was starting to get it, get it that Howard shot himself. How do we live through something like this? I still get so very, very tired when I think of all this, I really do.

I stood up straight and yelled for Luke to call 911, and then I heard the sound of him coming up the stairs. I turned away from Howard and left the bedroom, shutting the door behind me. No way was one of my children going to see this.

Luke had the phone in his hand and had already dialed, but no one was answering. I told him to give me the phone and get downstairs. I told him Daddy had had an accident with his gun. Luke listened and walked down the stairs, toward Trisha. I went out on the back porch and yelled for Craig next door to call 911.

I don't remember much after that.

*November 22, 2007*
*Thanksgiving Day*

*Hi Howie.*

*So here we are, at our first Thanksgiving without you.*

*I still find it unbelievable that you are gone. It's funny – people die every day all around us. It's a common event. Yet, when someone close to us dies, we find it just simply unbelievable that someone actually did die.*

*I want to try and make this my grief journal. I have no idea what it will include or say or lead to, but I want to try. Also, I will type it. I type so much faster than I write, and I believe I will stick to this if I type.*

*I think that fall is your season. All the smells remind me of you. You with your green vest on, walking (always slowly) through the leaves and grass. Remember when we used to hike up to Sugar Loaf Mountain every spring and fall? That was always nice.*

*You were a hard nut to crack, that was for sure. I guess I was just a nut, but we found each other. I always think back to when I saw you running at the high school. You called me over and sat with me and told me you were crazy about me and kissed me. You were so sweet and trusting and handsome, of course.*

*I miss you, Howie – with everything I have, I miss you! I hope when I ask Jesus to say hello to you, that He does. I keep asking for a definite sign that you are with Him in heaven – I haven't gotten it yet, but I still hold out hope.*

*Love, me*


*November 23, 2007*

*Hi Howard.*

*It is the day after Thanksgiving and I am having a really bad day. I just don't get why you had to do this. Well, I mean, I can* acknowledge all the pain you were in. I saw it in you over the years and saw it increase drastically over the past two years.

I just can't reconcile the fact that I couldn't make it better. I tried all different things. Some I know were not too helpful, like getting mad at you. But I saw deep down in you the potential to be happy and healthy. So many times you got close, but never for long. Was it what happened to you at age ten that wounded you beyond help?

I think of you each waking minute – every minute, all day, every day. I can't get you out of my mind and sometimes I think I am going out of my mind. This is so hard and so draining and so painful, I just don't know if I will come out the other side a whole person.

It's as if everyone in the world is standing on a dock in a lake, and the kids and I are suddenly thrown into the water. It is so very dark and foggy. At first, we can see everyone who is still on the dock. They are within arm's length and reaching out to us and sometimes touching our hands and hanging on. But they can never really pull us out of the lake. They try to pull us out, but they don't have enough strength or endurance.

As the weeks go by, we drift farther away from the dock. We don't want to, but the current takes us. It is so much colder away from the dock, and it gets darker and foggier. Trisha, Luke and I stay together in the water, very close to each other for warmth and support. We can only see certain people now on the dock – close family, some friends, some neighbors and a few others. They shout to us, ask us how we are. They cry sometimes, but mostly they just look on. There isn't much they can do as they are so far away.

It seems some people have left the dock and no longer reach out or make their presence known. I guess it is either too hard for them to keep staying there or else there are more pressing issues.

It seems there is a section of the lake for suicide survivors. This seems to be a remote part of the lake, farther from the dock and darker and scarier. I don't want to be here, and neither do the kids.

*I hope and pray we are, right now, as far away as we will ever be. I don't think we can handle being farther away from the dock and farther into the darkness of this lake. It is too cold, too scary, too deep. Treading water is taking its toll on all three of us.*

*We need God to reach out and pull us back in, but I cannot feel Him with us and I cannot feel you either, Howard. Where are you, God? Where are you, Howard? Why can't I sense you at all, Howard?*

*I am so sad, Howard. Were you this sad?*

*November 25, 2007*

*Hi Howard.*

*Today was once again just a horrible, painful day. I had to call my brother Jimmy as I needed reassurance that I would not die from a broken heart.*

*Lately I've found myself thinking of something and, for a few seconds, I think I've got to tell this to Howard or maybe call him on the phone. This used to happen a lot, but then it stopped. Now, all of a sudden, I've been doing it all week.*

*I remember you when we first met, down at the Chester Fire House. You were so sweet and handsome and smelled so good. I knew I loved you right then and there. Amazing, isn't it? To know right away. You had my heart and now you have broken it.*

*I don't think I can express in this journal the depth of my despair.*

*November 28, 2007*

*Hi Howard.*

*I could smell you today in the house. Not sure what it was (clothes maybe?), but I could tell it was the smell of you. So much* reminds me of you and makes for a lousy day when it all comes back. Geez, I wonder if I will ever feel okay again and not always sick to my stomach?

The kids and I went out with John last night. He came in from Colorado to visit and took us out to eat. It was great to listen to him tell the kids and me stories about you and him growing up. He is a big hunter and is blessed to be living in Colorado where he can hunt to his heart's content. I imagine that would have been the ideal place for you to be, with all that open space. I wish you could have escaped and moved out west like he did. I think it would have made you very happy.

I listened to John and put that together with all you told me and what I know of your family, and I got a small glimpse of the pain you were probably in for your whole life. I wish I could have removed all of that for you.

I think of someone like John and wonder if I will ever have someone in my life again to love? He is still single and seems very content with that and with what life has for him. I would love to get to that point – not worried about whether I have someone in my life.

Trisha made the basketball team! She worked very hard for it but then, once she made it, she complained of all the hard work it requires. I imagine nothing will happen easily for her during these teenaged years. Just when I think she is coming along and finding her groove, she erupts!

If Jesus can tell you, please pray for Trisha regarding her allergic reactions. They are so bad and life-threatening, and I just couldn't live with anything happening to her. Jesus, please ask God to help her, cure her and keep her and Luke alive until I die – and maybe let me live until my eighties – how's that?

Howard, I think of you walking on the streets of gold, walking and talking to Tyrone and to the baby we had first and lost. I know Tyrone gave you some heat over leaving me and the kids (if he was allowed to do that in heaven). He was always my biggest fan, you know that? Tell him I said hello and thanks for all his support and prayers. I wish he were still alive now so that I could talk to him about you and your suicide and heaven and whatever else. He would have been a great source of comfort and hope for me.

Got to go. My stomach is killing me – I never had a stomach problem until you died.

*December 04, 2007*

Hi Howard.

I have not written (typed) since November 28. Since that time, I went to Worker's Compensation court. Not much happened. There was a creepy little guy there, a wise ass. I almost said something to him, but I was overwhelmed. It was just too hard on me watching the judge's reaction when he found out you were dead.

He asked, "Is Mr. Nelson coming?" and the lawyer, Randy, had to say you were deceased. Then the judge read the death certificate with a look of horror on his face. He said he was sorry for my loss. I could barely say thanks.

I don't know, Howard. I hope and pray for Trisha and Luke. I worry Trisha will be boy crazy early and get into trouble just looking to fill that hole in her heart.

I asked God if perhaps it would help both kids if I find someone in the next year or two who is a Christian man who would take Trisha and Luke under his wing to guide them. That would be okay with me, Howard, and hopefully that doesn't make you mad. Then again, you're in heaven, so you won't be mad. Anyway, I am scared and fearful of having to raise them in their teen years all alone. A dad is what they need and you're not here for them.

I have no idea why I got on that subject – I guess I was thinking of Trisha as a young woman now, and it scares the hell out of me. At least with you here we could talk about it and plan things together for her to keep her steady. I have no idea what to do now.

*I have never sobbed and cried out like I did the other day. I thought I was losing my mind. I was beside myself. When I finally calmed down, I called Pastor Terryl who gave me some advice. I'm glad I finally reached out to him. It's hard for me to rely on others for emotional support. I don't know if it is because I am embarrassed or just scared.*

*Anyway, please ask Jesus to put a hedge of protection around this family, Howard, in place of you. Please ask Jesus to especially protect the kids and keep them safe during their teenage years. I need all the help I can get.*

*I just need to make it through this year and find some joy for the kids and me. I don't know what else to type or say.*

*Love you forever,*
*Your wife*

*December 06, 2007*

Hi Howie.

*We went to Manhattan today, to the doctor. We didn't find out exactly what is causing Trisha's anaphylactic reactions – however, she is highly allergic to grass!*

*No wonder she was diagnosed with asthma at twelve months old and just could never run outside. She couldn't breathe! They're putting her back on medication. I hope these breathing problems never return.*

*We got a cat two weeks ago. I imagine you are thrilled about that as you never liked cats. His name is Owen and he sleeps with Trisha.*

*I have no money coming in from your Worker's Compensation. I don't know if we will ever get money from them. I don't know much of anything anymore.*

*December 16, 2007*

*Hi Howard,*

*As you will see further down, I copied and pasted some items from the online Christian newsletter I get. Most of them this week were about worry, which I've done every day since you died. It was truly a blessing to have someone in my life who could carry at least some of the burden of worry.*

*I miss you, Howard. I miss hugging you and kissing you and lying next to you. I told Luke we should start a journal called Details About Dad and each of us write a few things we remember about you each week. His first thing was, "Dad's hands were always dirty!" I guess that is another way of saying you worked a lot.*

*If I had to write about what the kids and I are living these days, it would be one word – sadness. Being so sad for so long is so hard. It is physically and emotionally draining. And I still feel lost. I can't even get it together for Christmas dinner.*

*All the grief books say don't expect very much of yourself for at least a year. I have to tell you, Howard, these past seven months have felt like years. I hear people say how fast time is going, but I don't agree. It feels like it's been years and years that we have been sitting here grieving.*

*Dr. Klein says I am doing okay, but that's not good enough. How do I make decisions about work, money, whether or not to move. I just don't know where to begin.*

*I think of you in heaven so much. I wonder what you are doing and with whom. I'm stopping now. You know I love you, always loved you and forever will love you. I wonder if I will ever love again?*

*Jesus, please watch over Luke and Trisha and me and please can we have an easier week this week than last? PLEASE! Just some peace and rest and feeling of the Holy Spirit working in our hearts? Thank you.*

*Excerpts from the newsletter:*

*So I tell you, don't worry about everyday life—whether you have enough food, drink, and clothes. Can all your worry add a single moment to your life? Of course not. ... So don't worry about tomorrow, for tomorrow will bring its own worries. Today's trouble is enough for today!'*

*– Matthew 6:25-34 NLT*

*Worry is the interest paid on trouble before it falls due.*

*– Author Unknown*

*It is not work that kills men; it is worry. Worry is rust upon the blade.*

*– Henry Ward Beecher*


*December 20, 2007*

*Dear Howard,*

*The other day, I was thinking of when we were dating and we were in the Monroe park. I told you I didn't want to see you anymore. It was November, I think. You had on a softball jacket – a kind of ugly, shiny blue one. You had hair then – curly and dark brown.*

*You touched the ends of my hair and you were twirling it between your fingers. I think that is when I fell in love with you. You were so kind and gentle and soft.*

*How is heaven? Do you see us? Do you know what we are doing and feeling? Does Jesus give you any reports about us? Do you miss us up there? I guess not; if there are no tears or pain in heaven then you cannot be missing us.*

*Grief is hard and cold.*

*Love forever,*

*Your wife*

*December 21, 2007*

Hi Howard.

Four more days until Christmas. You are with Jesus – what an awesome Christmas you'll have!

As always, I miss you terribly. I think of you years ago. I remember one frigid, cold January before we had kids, when we were living in that small two-room house on Scotchtown Avenue. I came home from work in a cab, and the driver dropped me off before I realized I didn't have any keys.

I waited for a while for you. Cell phones weren't in use yet. (Imagine that.) It was about six degrees. Finally, you came home from a bar, drunk. I remember being so damn annoyed. I think I threw something at you.

The next day I went to the Laundromat. You came over to meet me, and I wasn't talking to you. You sat down next to me and, once again, started playing with my hair. That would always soften me, and I guess you knew that.

You looked right into my eyes and said, "I missed you, you know," and of course I melted. I just wanted us to be good together – nice to each other and intimate.

I love you. I pray, however, that I can find someone to be intimate with who is stable. I don't know about me, though. I must have lousy self-esteem. But you loved me, and that was enough. I loved that you loved me. Funny, huh?

Jesus, please be with us three as this holiday comes. Please don't make it too sad or tiresome. Tell Howard I love him and the kids miss him so, so, so much! And, Jesus, make sure you tell Howard hello right now. Thanks.

Howard, bye for now. Love you and always will.

You were so damn sexy!!!!!!!!

*December 25, 2007*
*Christmas Day*

*Christmas Day, Howard, and the first one without you. I don't know how this will go or what we will do.*

*Not good. This just isn't good. The kids are not doing well in school and I think the three of us are just so tired of being sad and devastated. Jesus, please be with us.*

*Merry Christmas in heaven, Howard. I'm not feeling too fond of you right now, so this is a short note.*

*Love always,*
*Me*


*December 30, 2007*

*Hi Howard.*

*Almost the end of the worst year of my life. I still get short of breath at times when I think you are dead.*

*This is such a long, dark and lonely winter, Howard. How are you? Are you truly walking with Jesus? Is Tyrone walking with you?*

*I know he was a firm believer in Jesus and I do miss him here. If he were still alive when you killed yourself, he would have been my greatest supporter. I so very much wish he were here for me to talk to about you.*

*Howard – I don't want to think of the pain you were in all your life. I hope I helped give you some joy, you know? That would make it all worthwhile, if you could tell me when we meet again that, yes, I gave you some happiness.*

*Howard, I STILL don't know what I am going to do without you here.*

*December 31, 2007*
*New Year's Eve*

Hi Howard.

The last day of 2007 – I am certainly not sorry to see this year go. However, in letting it go, you have been away longer and get even further away. I pray that Luke and Trisha had you here long enough to know there is a God and they can believe in Him.

God, do you step in even more for children with no father? I pray you do.

Howard, I know your 2008 and forever after will be beautiful beyond imagination. I cannot say that for us. Please pray to Jesus for us, for strength and faith and wisdom for the kids as they go through their teenage years. And all of that for me as I try to raise them! I hate being alone.

Forever yours but hopefully someday I may belong to someone else again!

Love,
Your wife


*January 30, 2008*

Hi Howard.

It has been one month since I have written and a lot has happened. I finally got my knee replacement – wish you were here to see it and help me through it. It's been so very hard without you here during this time. I keep wondering what you do each day. Lately, all I do is sit at home. Obviously my knee surgery is a bit of a setback. It was hard enough being alone so much even when I could walk the dogs and go to the gym – but now being alone and immobile is killing me.

Pastor Terryl called the other day. It was on a day I was going to call him as it was a very hopeless day for me, and there he was on the answering machine. He must have sensed my need to talk to him. It is such good medicine to talk to a man who has walked with God for a long, long time.

I guess I am still a little po'd with God – not for your suicide, but for His not intervening very much since then (i.e. worker's comp money). But I know deep in my heart He is there – too many people have entered my life and have helped me for it to be anything else but God's handiwork. Still, I try so hard not to worry about the future, but I haven't been too successful at that.

I thought of you today and what it will be like when I die and see you! But I was a little sad because supposedly no one is married in heaven, and I want to still be married to you there! I want to be your special someone even up in heaven, and I feel so sad to think that is not how it will be.

Do you think of us? Do you even know of us and what we are currently doing down here? Just how does it work in heaven? Does Jesus give you updates on us?

Howard, please know I am sorry for any time I was mean or not understanding. I mean it – it breaks my heart to think of the times I just didn't get it, and I pray you can forgive me. Please. I love you – have always loved you and will forever love you.

February 06, 2008

Hi Howard.

Well, I had my forty-sixth birthday this past weekend – February 3 in case you forgot. I wonder if you knew about it in heaven? Do you have any recognition of us down here and what we are doing? Or are you gone completely for now?

It has been dreary, rainy and ugly for almost the past two and a half months. What an ugly, ugly winter. Even in normal circumstances it would be a hard winter to get through, but with you gone it comes close to impossible. Eight and a half months later, and I'm still just cleaning and sitting in the house.

I don't know how to get out of this rut. I think sunny weather may help, but that means I have to wait until at least April. Diane and Jimmy and Pastor Terryl tell me it takes baby steps and that baby steps are okay at this point. I may go to the firehouse this Saturday. I haven't been there since your funeral. Supposedly a group is getting together and Louie told me about it.

The dogs still miss you, Howie – I can tell. Sometimes Diesel just lies there with this look in his eyes. You let a lot of people down by leaving the way you did. I never thought the kids or I would have to live with something like this. Most days, I still shake my head in bewilderment and confusion and sadness.

Well, I've got to go, Howie. Please know if I could give you a big kiss and hug I would. I miss you, Howard, more than you could ever know.

Love, Me

February 11, 2008

Hi Howard.

It's soooo cold today – almost ten below this morning with the wind. How I hate these days.

The lawyer called the other day. She said there is no chance really for a malpractice suit because in your counselor records you state you would never kill yourself because of your love for your wife and kids and religion.

What the hell happened? What happened that day that I didn't notice? I am so sorry if it was me. If only we could go back and do this over, Howard.

The depression is back and I am having such a hard time. It feels like there is just no way out. Right now I feel like lying in the bed and doing nothing. Not thinking, not believing, not hoping. Just me and the kids lying in the bed and wasting away.

Got to go. This is too painful today.

February 18, 2008

Hi Howard.

Still waiting for my sign. Some days I don't ask for it; other days I do. I know some day Jesus will show me something unmistakable that will demonstrate that you are with Him and He is with us.

You know, Howard, I miss you – I miss hugging you and kissing your face. I miss your smell. I guess I just miss everything about you. You were my first love. I was so damn crazy for you. You made me feel very sexy, you know that? Wish I could have been so much more for you, Howard – I really wish I could have.

Bye for now, Howard. Love you and always will.

Your wife

February 18, 2008

*Love is a fabric that never fades, no matter how often it is washed in the waters of adversity and grief.*

– Author Unknown

Dear God.

I remember a poster on a dorm room wall during college. The poster had a picture of a homeless man lying in a dirty gutter holding a bottle in a paper bag. The inscription was a quote from Mother Teresa: "You love Jesus only as much as the person you love the least."

For all we don't understand about the life of Jesus and the true nature of you, God, there is one truth that is completely clear. The Christian faith is about service and humility. It's about helping *those who can't help themselves. It's about loving others more than we love ourselves – even the most unlovable among us.*

*What is the sign of true followers? Is it the amount of knowledge that we have? Is it the money we give to missions? The degrees we've earned? The number of people we've preached to? The hours we've spent worshiping in church? The books we've read or written?*

*It is said that when Francis of Assisi left his wealth behind to seek you, he stripped naked and walked out of the city. The first person he encountered on his journey was a leper on the side of the road. He first passed him, then turned back. He embraced the leper in his arms before continuing his journey. A few steps down the road he turned and saw that the leper was gone.*

*Until his dying day, Francis of Assisi was convinced that the leper was Jesus. Even if he was wrong, he was right.*

*Even though we miss Howard terribly, God, and his leaving us was the worst thing to have ever had happened to this family, I pray that Trisha, Luke and I will always extend love to those around us; especially, as you say, those deemed unlovable. I know that is what you would want from us, God.*

*Jesus, please be with Trisha and Luke and me as we go through this week. You also know I need to do something about work. Help me pray and wait for your hand to work in that area, and may you be guiding what happens with the lawsuit and Worker's Compensation.*

*Thank you for hearing our prayers, Jesus!*

*February 18, 2008*

*Hi Howard.*

*You were very much missed this past Valentine's Day.*

*I know Trisha missed you terribly. She missed her rose and card from her dad.*

*February 24, 2008*

Hi Howard.

Another cold day. Another day the furnace isn't working.

I read the card you gave me with flowers last year on our twentieth anniversary. It says, "I wish you the best in life – I love you really really really."

Well, really really really, if you wished me the best in life, Howard, you wouldn't have killed yourself. Our hearts are broken, just like the furnace.

But, life keeps going on. It's weird. I don't have an interest in anything, don't know if I ever will. But each day we three get up and shower, the kids go to school and I clean.

I'm reading a book now that deals with "feeling it." We aren't suppose to go by our feelings as they can lead us astray. Feelings are very fleeting and often exaggerated and can be influenced by so many things – weather, hormones, food and so on. This book says to just trust and continue believing what God has written. I'm trying but I have to tell you, a little concrete evidence would go a long way.

Howard, how are you? I miss you more these days than a few months ago, which I find odd. I keep looking at your pictures. I found a beautiful one of you at the beach about one year before all your back surgeries started. You're holding a baseball glove and looking at the camera – what the heck happened, Howard? How did it get so bad that you couldn't tell me what you were thinking?

Just to give you a kiss you on your head one more time – boy, would I love that! And to hold your hand. I loved holding hands.

Got to go – Diesel wants to go out again. This single parenting stuff is for the birds.

Love,

Your wife

March 04, 2008

Hi Howard.

I stopped by the firehouse the other day. First time since you died. Louie was there and took me around.

Sergio wrote a tribute to you and had it framed and hung it by your picture. I couldn't read it as I started crying, so I don't know what it says.

Luke and Trisha are trying out for baseball/softball these next two weeks. Please Jesus, help them make the teams!

And Jesus if you can, please tell Howard about the kids and what they are doing. I'm not sure how it works up there, but I'll just go on the assumption that you can tell Howard things for us, okay?

I'm still so lost, Howard. Don't know which way to turn. I'm cooking more, which Luke loves, but I just can't seem to get it together. I guess in time, but I have no idea.

Still hoping God comes through with an idea or plan on work. We need the money.

March 04, 2008

I used to say the Prayer of Jabez. One line in it was "Enlarge our territories." I don't pray that anymore. I don't want my territories or Luke's or Trisha's to be enlarged anymore. They were enlarged last May when Howard killed himself, and it is too painful.

Yes, many people came out and listened to Pastor Terryl and received the true message, but for that to happen our lives had to be destroyed. That's a pretty high price to pay for such a message to be delivered.

This grief is so heavy, so smothering. I imagine Howard's was, too, before he killed himself. I wonder, if I feel this terrible pain but don't wish to kill myself, just how much worse did Howard feel because he did want to kill himself?

*I must forgive him when I consider the pain he was in, but why couldn't God heal his pain without letting him kill himself? I wonder if I will ever forgive God for that? Howard died, and I feel as if I died, too – what good can come from that, Lord?*

*When I think of turning away from a God who could allow someone as sad and desperate as Howard to kill himself, I then have to think of the alternative – which is what? The alternative would be to turn toward this world and the things of this world that rot and rust. Not much of an alternative, is it?*

*I guess I'll keep looking towards the God who says He loves us, that He will never forsake us, that He is our protector and comforter. I'll just sit here and wait for all He has written to actually come true.*

*I'm waiting, God. Help me see it and know it and believe it.*

*March 09, 2008*

*Hi Howard.*

*The rain continues. It's been raining for four and a half months now. Luke made the high school JV baseball team. But of course you are not here to celebrate. You have left us high and dry.*

*You can probably tell how mad I am at you. I don't know if I will ever fully forgive you. You have ruined our lives, that's for sure. I need to find someone or something that will help me get my energy and hope back – you took it away the day you pulled that trigger. Did death bring the relief you were looking for?*

*I've got to go. I am too sad to even want to type to you right now.*

*March 10, 2008*

*I really don't feel like doing this anymore.*

# 10

## Teen Grief

My father never killed himself, so I wouldn't presume to know how my kids felt when theirs did.

But I can guess.

There was Luke, fourteen years old and heading to high school at the end of that terrible summer after his father shot himself up in the bedroom. Walking through those doors into high school is traumatic enough even if your father is home sitting at the dinner table every night.

I don't know how he survived. I do know he shut down for three years –verbally, emotionally and physically.

There was Trisha, just having turned thirteen. I remember being thirteen. I felt fat, ugly, incompetent, ridiculous and lonesome all at once. And I had a father.

Entering eighth grade can actually be kind of nice, though. Suddenly you're one of the oldest kids in the middle school – you've earned some liberties and privileges and the right to feel a bit superior. You are seasoned, wiser, smarter and more confident.

And there was my daughter, a girl who had just lost her best friend, the man she loved more than anyone else in the world. He was the parent she truly identified with, and he was *gone*. Gone by his own hand. He actually up and left her, and she was only twelve years old.

And there I was – the single mother of two teenagers. Two *new* teenagers – kids who were just starting to go through adolescence and all that comes with it. How would I ever get them – and me – through to the other side undamaged?

As I write these words years later, I still get sick to my stomach. I feel the adrenaline surging and the rise of panic, despair and fear. My children are eighteen and twenty as I sit here typing, yet when I think about the beginning of our new lives together, I feel what I felt then.

It still takes my breath away. It still makes me search for a way out.

Even in an average family with average kids, parents can expect chaos and worry to come knocking at the door as the kids approach their teens. There are surging hormones and the emergence of sexual feelings, the desire to pierce or tattoo some body part, school pressure, feelings of inadequacy and not fitting in, outbursts of anger and frustration, broken down cars, temper tantrums over the word *no*, alcohol and drugs, and confusion.

Everyone is confused – parents, kids, even the family pets.

I faced all of that, of course. It's a basic part of raising kids. But in the shadow of their father's death, basic problems became devastating. In fact, things were so terrible that I think we've all developed a bit of amnesia about that first school year after Howard died, when Luke was in ninth grade and Trisha was in eighth.

That fall I was still home. I had taken a year off from work largely because I was in no condition to keep a job, keep tabs on the kids and keep sane. The life insurance would be used to get the three of us through the first year.

So there I was, at home and able to concentrate my worry on the kids. And it was Trisha who worried me most.

There was one stark difference between Luke and Trisha. Luke had a few close friends who were present in his life, Jared in particular. Jared came to our house almost every day after school. He didn't say much. He didn't place any demands on anyone. He simply was.

He walked home with Luke, then both he and Luke would immediately use the bathrooms. Apparently they were both opposed to using the high school bathrooms, so they were very eager to get to the john when they got home. I wondered why, but I never asked.

Jarad played XBox and PlayStation with Luke. He took it upon himself to take out the garbage. He talked to me, but I doubt he and Luke ever spoke of Howard. He was a constant presence in our lives and a tremendous source of comfort for both Luke and me.

Some kids in Luke's life had parents who coached them on how to be a good friend to Luke. For this I am eternally grateful. Luke was quiet throughout high school, but those friends and families who reached out to include him made all the difference for him.

Still, Luke was shutting down. For two years, he didn't smile, talk or show much emotion. Both the kids were in counseling – we tried several different therapists. Luke had contempt for them all and claimed he was able to fool them. He told them everything was okay, and he said they went along with the masquerade. I don't know whether or not that's true, but clearly everything was *not* okay.

Still, on the face of it, he seemed to be handling life better than his sister.

* * *

His sister. My lonesome Trisha. Perhaps eighth graders are too young to be that devoted, that consistent in their friendship. I don't know – perhaps it was a girl thing? Girls mature faster than boys, so the girls in eighth grade were heading into puberty. Perhaps having a friend such as Trisha with her huge grief, sadness and detachment wasn't something they could handle. Maybe it gobbled too much of their fun.

I know she had one friend in particular, Lindsay Jackson, who tried so hard to be there for Trisha. I can't imagine the burden Lindsay carried, listening to Trisha's profound sadness and to her silences. It must have been exhausting for her. And it probably just couldn't go on without sapping Lindsay's own happiness.

Whatever the cause, Trisha's experience that first year and during the remainder of the time she stayed in high school was much lonelier than Luke's.

I have often thought of this and cannot figure it out. Why would Luke's friends rally around him while Trisha most often found herself alone? Luke had sports, and I suppose that helped. Bonding seems to happen naturally among teammates. But Trisha removed herself from all sports and extracurricular activities. She was not on a team of any sort.

When Trisha moved on to high school, her ability to handle the daily drama of school life was severely limited. She just couldn't do the teenager thing. She had no interest in the usual gossip – who talked to whom in the hallway, who gossiped about whom at lunch and on Facebook, who spread rumors about whom after each party and dance.

I wanted so much for Trisha to call a girlfriend and maybe go shopping or hang out. I wanted so much for her to go to the school dance, the homecoming game, the powder puff football game. It didn't happen. She didn't attend her prom, she didn't go to class day, she didn't go on the senior trip, she wasn't included in many birthday parties and celebrations, and she missed most of those girl trips to the mall.

Gradually, the friends she had known for years stopped calling her. I often wonder which of us was more crushed by this. I wish someone had reached out to her despite her inability to be engaged, but no one really did. It broke my heart.

Little by little, she isolated herself. Little by little, she was ignored at school – at times, even made fun of. Can you imagine being ridiculed because you are struggling with your dad's suicide? I can never forgive their meanness. It was so damaging.

By the middle of her sophomore year, Trisha left high school and attended night classes instead. She would eventually get her high school diploma, but she never got high school.

Nearly every bump in the road – boulders, really – caused me to over-react. I liked to think I was able to go with the flow sometimes, but obviously I didn't do that very often. The kids frequently told me to stop freaking out about things, to stop worrying so much.

Of course I worried. My deepest concern was that they would see suicide as an option for their own pain and depression. After all, it was their father's solution.

So of *course* I freaked out. A lot.

I remember telling my counselor, Gail, about a panic attack I had after once leaving Luke and Trisha home alone for six hours. This was *two years* after Howard's suicide. They were fifteen and sixteen, and we all had telephones. But I had a panic attack.

"Trish," Gail said. "Of course you fear leaving them alone. The last time you left someone alone – someone who was depressed and sad – you came home to find him dying on the floor after shooting himself."

It finally clicked for me. And I finally sat down with the kids to tell them that this was my fear for them and that, yes, it was a genuine fear because it had already happened once to me. I had to own up to it and allow the kids to know it.

This caused them more pain, I know, but it also allowed us to work together toward helping Mommy with this one.

And I did have my own maturing to do. I had to learn to accept that my children would not have normal teenage years. It was probably similar to what parents of a special needs child go through – their child is different, and the situation is out of their control. Parents can't force other children to be friends with their own different child.

Part of my own growing up occurred when I backed off and allowed Trisha to make many of the decisions that shaped her high school experience. I tried to follow Trisha's lead, and so did the school counselors.

I began working with her to build experiences to match what *she* wanted, what *she* could handle and what was going to be the best thing for *her*. It was a loss for sure – yet another one in a long line of losses.

But it was what it was.

*  *  *

For both of them, though, there was only one major decision to be made during those first two years after their father's death – to get out of bed every morning and go through the motions of living. There was no joy in their lives, and there was very little emotion of any kind. They both took along with them a suitcase filled with grief whenever they left the house.

My children had shut down. They didn't grow emotionally or psychologically during that period. They stopped maturing on the inside. In some respects, they were stuck for a while at the age they were the day their father left them.

Picture yourself at the cusp of adolescence facing the overwhelming task of having to grow and mature while you carry the heavy burden of your father's suicide. Trying to become the best version of yourself without tragedy in your life is difficult enough, but this? This??

When Howard took his own life, he took part of his children's spirit and soul along with him. I truly believe that. And if I had to identify the one thing that still produces anger in me toward Howard, this is it.

Oddly enough, both of my kids stayed out of trouble throughout their first three years of high school. I think it was because they had shut down. They had very little interest in partying, drinking, drugging. It was, weirdly, the one positive result of their acute sadness.

We did, however, suffer through other events that I would gladly have traded for the normal torture that most parents experience at the hands of their teenagers. As honest and open as I have been on these pages, there are some stories I have no right to share. Those stories belong to my children. The telling is for them to decide.

Their grief was solely their own, too. As much as I wanted to protect them from it, my job was to *not* help them avoid it. I couldn't fix what happened. I couldn't save them from the inevitable. I had to let them feel what they needed to feel. I had to allow them to move into those dark places so that they could eventually move out of them.

Do you know how hard it is to allow your children to feel such extreme sadness, loss and devastation? Think of how hurt you feel for your kid when he simply can't hit the ball off the damn T. Their pain overwhelmed me with fear. What if they killed themselves because they could not cope with it?

And sometimes the solicitous concern from family and friends was no help. Teenagers are quieter with the adults in their lives by nature, so having two teens who had lost their dad pull into their own shells falls within the range of normal on the scale of things – if anything about this might be considered normal.

But it was so hard to be asked, "Are you sure they're okay?"

No, for crying out loud, I wasn't sure! I was doing the best I could, but when it came right down to it, I couldn't be one hundred percent sure, could I? And neither could anyone else.

But there were those who wanted me to satisfy their own fears that, yes, I knew exactly what I was doing and it would be okay. I couldn't make that promise to anyone, least of all myself. I only could stay vigilant and make decisions with love.

It wasn't until the third year out for Luke and the fourth for Trisha that my lost children started to re-emerge, to regain their personalities and re-start their emotional growth.

They'd had a long timeout and, for quite a while, they would be behind their peers in their development.

\* \* \*

I have pictures of both my children before Howard died. Their smiles and eyes are so alive and filled with light that the photos seem to glow.

And I have pictures – far too many – of my kids after Howard died. Their eyes are dead pools of sadness and loneliness. There is no light, there are no smiles.

Those pictures break my heart. When I look at them, I make almost a physical movement to get away from the place those pictures bring me. I know if I stay there looking at their faces, imagining all they might be feeling – or *not* feeling – I could spiral downward to a point from which I could not recover.

It's as if I'm climbing down one of those ladders that access the street sewers, like in the movie *The Fugitive*. As I look at the deadness in my kids' eyes, I am traveling down one of those ladders and I'm looking at dark, filthy, fast-moving water that could sweep me away.

If I stay in the place that imagines all the hurt, despondency, loss and devastation this suicide has caused my children, I would surely descend further down that ladder and, at some point, fall into the current and be swept away.

# 11

## Trisha Speaks
*Sad Eye, Happy Eye*

My father had been gone from me for two years when I drew the self-portrait you'll see when you turn the page.

I was fourteen at the time, and I was trying to be happy. But being happy was so very, very hard. I didn't really succeed at it all that well.

The picture expresses the conflicting emotions I was feeling then, toward my father and toward life itself. I think the fact that I put Luke and my mom inside the heart on my left cheek and I put my dad just outside of it might best express how I felt about him at that time.

I just didn't know where to put him in my heart – or my head. Sometimes I still don't.

Here's the poem I wrote to go with the picture.

> Never forgotten,
> Never left,
> Always in my mind.
> You left me behind.
>
> Forever loved,
> Forever hated.
> Always hoping,

Con't on page 112

## *Closing Eyes on a Dark Past, Opening Them to a Brighter Future*

*Trisha's self-portrait as she saw herself at the age of 14*

*Trisha*

Always wishing.
Looking at your grave
With tears holding back.
Trying to be brave.

That cold stare
Reminds me of
Those life-changing days.

Never said goodbye.
Take the bullet of death
To dodge the bullet of life.
It was heart-breaking,
But step by step
I'm putting it back
Together.

Made me stronger,
Made me better.
Found myself,
My true self, after.

Growing without you is tough,
I miss your love.
You're eternally happy,
I'm forever sad.

It showed how you
Were a coward.
Yeah,
I'm mad.

But I'll forever
Love you,
Dad.

*Lo, I am with you always, even unto the end of the age.*

Matthew 28:20

# 12

## Grief Journal
### *The First Year, Con't*

*March 2008*

### Some Things I've Learned So Far

*Howard's suicide is like those TVs with a picture in a picture. Some days his suicide is the big picture and my life is the small picture up in the top left corner. Other times, his suicide is the small picture in the corner and my life is the bigger picture. I hope, as days go by, his death will be the smaller picture more often than not. I can hope.*

*My timing and God's timing are completely different. My job is to figure out how to live with God's timing without always jumping ahead with some small amount of patience.*

*It's okay to hurry up and wait. The hurrying part makes me feel like I'm accomplishing something.*

*Sometimes God wants me to do nothing – honest to God! If He puts nothing in front of me but the dishes, the laundry, the driving to and fro, and the meals, then it is quite possible that is ALL He expects of me that day.*

"Everybody Loves Raymond" has brought a smile to my face and a hearty laugh from my belly. I guess there's hope if there's a laugh or two.

I've never before experienced such gut-wrenching, painful, almost deadly sobbing that I have gone through with Howard's death. And, although I thought it would kill me, I lived through the sobbing. I still find that amazing.

I have never felt so intensely as this past year. Not a state I wish to be in forever. There is something to be said for turning it all off and just sitting there watching "Everybody Loves Raymond."

Donate your organs! Donate your family's organs! Trust me on this one.

Supportive, funny, reliable families are not the rule; they're the exception. My family is among my greatest blessings.

My childhood friends mean the world to me. I already knew this but it was reinforced again and again this past year.

Fellow parishioners from your church do pray for you like they say they will and it makes all the difference in the world. The prayers of the faithful are what get us out of the bed every morning. I know that to be true.

My kids and I live on a nice street, with nice neighbors, in a nice town, in a beautiful state and in a free country. There's a lot to be said for that.

Dogs make the nights easier and softer (and hairier).

My kids have spirit and a genuine desire to have fun inside them that keeps me going. Their resilience, courage, character and stamina are beyond words.

*March 2008*

## Some Practical Things I've Learned So Far

How to actually charge the battery in my car. I had to do it twice in one week.

*How to remove, clean and then replace the filter in the bathroom ceiling vent. I looked up the other day and saw this black stuff coating the outside of the vent. I climbed up and figured out how to get the darn thing off without breaking it. After that it was easy.*

*I figured out last fall how to mix the gas and oil for the leaf blower. They actually sell pre-measured oil for this right downtown at the hardware store. Who knew?*

*In addition to mixing the gas and oil, I even found the spark plug, pulled it out, cleaned it and put it back in. I'm not sure if I'll remember how to do it this coming fall, though.*

*The toilets decided to give me trouble this year. I guess they felt left out while I was cleaning the ceiling vent. I can adjust the float now and that rubber stopper thing.*

*The ground hogs have been a challenge. The big rock in the hole didn't work. Any advice in that area would be greatly appreciated.*

*I've learned the difference between a Phillips head screwdriver and the other one; that there really is a 3/16th wrench; that a level helps when hanging something; that it is useful to read the directions when putting together the computer chair; and that I really can call someone when I'm stuck.*

*I can get on the roof and replace the section of vinyl siding that blew off the house during the winter.*

*This list keeps getting longer and longer. I just figured out how to remove the furnace filter, go buy the right-sized new one and put it in. Wonders never cease.*

*March 11, 2008*

Hi Howard.

*Spring is about ten days away now, and I think of last spring. That's when your friend Kevin died. Maybe killed himself. It was around March 22, 2007. Is that when you started to think about* it? I just cannot fathom the back pain being that bad – I mean I knew you hurt, but was it more than that? It had to have been. You began to get crankier and more withdrawn the summer of 2005 I think – around the time Chili died.

I'm so messed up from you and our twenty tumultuous years together and now your suicide. Will someone ever come into my life who is pulled together and bring me some joy? I have this sinking feeling I am screwed.

I don't want to end up alone for another thirty or forty years, but you know what? Looking at how unfaithful so many men are today, I don't think I'll meet someone who could commit and stay involved. Just today we heard that our New York governor, Eliot Spitzer, was busted for being involved in a prostitution ring. He paid about $4,600 to be with a hooker for three hours. And you have to see his wife! She is gorgeous, and they say she is a sweetheart. He has three daughters, I believe.

What in the world are normal girls like me going to do? If someone as smart, successful and attractive as she is has a husband who pays thousands to sleep with another woman, what hope is there for people like me? What in the world is wrong with guys like this? Are they that selfish they risk everything that has any value in their lives just so they can get laid? It's not like this is a rare occurrence. It happens all the time. Internet porn is worth billions of dollars. Obviously someone is paying for it.

Back to why I even brought this up – am I so naïve to believe that there is such a thing as commitment and that some men still want it? I had you, but you pulled away years ago into your own shell. No, you didn't cheat on me, but you weren't part of my life in many ways.

Is God watching all this? Is there any hope for me today, Lord? Howard, any chance Jesus tells you hello for us? If He does, I hope He tells you about Luke. He cut off all his beautiful curls – it killed me to watch! He is so darn handsome, and his eyes are the bluest blue. Girls are going to fall all over him!

March 12, 2008

## I Think I'm On The Wrong Bus

*It's as if the bus suddenly stopped with a violent jerk*
*You get thrown completely out of your seat*
*No chance to even grab hold of something or someone*
*Wildly flailing arms; legs off the ground*
*Eyes wide open; throat closed but you want to scream*
*Heart feels as if it is not beating*
*When in fact it is beating without order*
*You would give anything to recognize something normal*
*Something familiar and safe*
*But no such luck*
*This sudden, violent stop of the bus has sent you flying*

*Funny though, you never seem to land*
*You keep flying around the inside of that bus*
*Arms, legs, hair all in disarray*
*Your mind trying to make sense of what is around you*
*Windows don't look like windows*
*And the faces of those near you are blurred and fleeting*

*This is what life becomes from the moment you find out*
*Someone you love has killed himself*
*It's violent, it's abrupt, it's as if someone has turned you*
*Inside out and then removed gravity from your life*

*I'm waiting for the bus to at least slow down*
*Perhaps then I can grab hold of something or someone*
*Grabbing hold will give me hope –*
*Never thought how precious hope is*
*It would even make the basic a little easier to handle*
*HOPE – it's like a jewel to me at this point*
*Precious, unique and desired*

*March 15, 2008*

## Toilet Paper

*I was looking for a roll of toilet paper and got to thinking about how I like it to be hung a certain way. The thought hit me that at least I can determine which way the toilet paper gets to hang. It has to unroll from the front, not the back.*

*This is important because we actually have very little control over our lives. Controlling how the toilet paper hangs somehow makes me feel that I do, in fact, have some measure of control; otherwise I would be hard pressed to continue.*

*March 17, 2008*

Dear Howard.

Happy St. Patrick's Day to you, Howard. How are you up there in heaven? We still miss you, even in our sleep.

Trisha keeps two of your T-shirts preserved. She has one in her pillow case at all times and another in a plastic storage box so that the smell of you is always there.

Watching Luke walk away from the car to go into school is so painful. I see the back of him and how tall he has gotten and how much he walks like you. Well, the you when you had a healthy back and moved fast. I wonder if his heart breaks every time he sees a dad with his son playing ball.

Luke and Trisha and I – we're forever changed. We are no longer the people we were last May 27, 2007, the day before you shot yourself. How do I rebuild and redefine myself at age forty-six? I have no idea. Right now I take each day as it comes. I work first on getting out of the bed. On school days, getting out of the bed at six a.m. is not so bad because I do it for the kids. They need me to get them up and get them to school. It is after they leave the house that I have such a difficult time.

*We have some very difficult days coming up. Your birthday, a trip to Florida, our twenty-first anniversary, Mother's Day, the day you shot yourself, the day you died, the day we buried you, Father's Day. Overwhelming.*

*Bye for now, Howard. If you can, please somehow let Trisha and Luke know you're always with them, okay Howard?*

*March 17, 2008*

*Hi Again Howard.*

*The gentleman who received your liver called last week. I spoke to him and his wife. Their names are Cavana and Marlene. They are so grateful for the organ donation, and they swear you still live on and are not far away from me or Trisha or Luke.*

*I really would like to believe that. That you are close by and Jesus allows you to know about us and pray for us and still be a part of our lives in some way.*

*I wonder what you would say to me if I showed up in heaven right now? Or if I could get a glimpse of you up there, what would I see?*

*I wish I could have given you some of that happiness here on earth and maybe then you wouldn't have killed yourself.*

*Killed yourself – I don't know if I always knew this would happen or not. I wonder what we know deep, deep down but cannot acknowledge or come to terms with? You were always so sad, agitated and depressed, you know? Wish I could have changed that for you.*

*Got to go. Writing to you and about you is very difficult some days.*

*Love you!*

*March 23, 2008*
*Easter Morning*

*Hi Howard.*

*Good morning to my husband. I imagine in heaven you don't need a special day to celebrate that Jesus died and rose again. He is Risen – He is risen indeed.*

*I guess I don't have to tell you that another holiday without you isn't going to make for a good day. The kids and I kind of just plug along, doing what needs to be done, but that's about it.*

*Trisha is still so, so sad and angry. I try to talk to Luke about what he is feeling, but he gets annoyed with me and would rather cry in his room alone. I hope that, in the end, he won't suffer more in the future because he didn't grieve right today. Not right in the sense of right and wrong, but right for him.*

*I still struggle with why you would do this to us – leave us completely alone. Actually you abandoned us. Was it something I did? Something I said? It seems you blame me somewhat, especially since you left the letter I wrote to you on our anniversary right there next to your suicide note. What were you thinking? Stupid question – obviously you weren't thinking. Not about us, anyway; just about getting out of here, I guess.*

*I am coming to a realization, Howard, that is so depressing. One never, ever gets over a suicide. You just don't get over IT. IT never gets better, and IT never goes away. You just learn to live with IT, as if you have to a chronic disease. The thought of living with IT day after day for the rest of my life drains me.*

*And how do you find happiness living with IT? How do you give to others while you are busy living with IT? Where do you put IT when you go to work or to someone else's house or out to dinner and a movie? Or even just sitting out front on the steps – you always have to make room for IT. Where do you put IT? Why can't you just leave IT out in the back yard for a day?*

*Thanks, Howard, for giving IT to me and Trisha and Luke – IT was not a gift we wanted and I wonder, did you ever consider how IT was going to affect our lives forever and ever?*

March 24, 2008

*I just heard today from SueAnn in the staff development office at Good Sam that they will not give me the per diem job. I applied for it weeks ago as it was two days per week and enough per hour that I could forfeit the Social Security for me.*

*I have no idea whether I was hoping for it or not. I have no idea what to hope for anymore. For crying out loud, what the hell am I going to do? I have two teenagers and a house and no job. If I work full time then there is no one here to drive them around. I just don't know what to do with this position Howard has put us in. I can't even get up enough energy today to be mad at him.*

*God, PLEASE can you help us? Can you intervene either in the shape of a job for me or something wonderful in our lives? Or peace or something? Maybe a sign from you, God, that everything will be okay? You've got to help me believe that you are really in control, God. I have not heard from you or seen any sign that you are.*

*Each day just goes by and I get more depressed and lonely. How useful will I be for these kids? I have very little talent and I really doubt I can juggle all of this.*

*How in the world did Howard think things would be better for us if he was gone? How could he possibly think that by killing himself he was giving us a better life? For crying out loud, he left me with two beautiful kids who now have a dad who killed himself and a mom who has no job and is despondent.*

*God, I am crying out to you. Please, will you answer?*

March 26, 2008

Hi Howard.

I started looking at the stuff in the basement and shed that you left me with. I could choke you when I look at all this stuff! What the heck am I going to do with it all? I can't even lift half of it.

There must be three air compressors, heaven knows how many welders, rakes, chain saws, shovels, jacks, ropes, chains, saws, a million tools. The task of cleaning all this out is too overwhelming – I think I will ask my dad and Jimmy to devote two days to helping me. I just don't have the energy.

Spring just started. Now when I think of spring, I think of you and last year of course. How Luke was in the middle of baseball season and so was Trisha. How you killed yourself right in the middle of their busiest season.

I don't know how I will handle all their games this year without you here. At the very least, you went to the games. I feel a great loneliness just thinking of sitting at those games alone – watching each of them hit and run with you nowhere to be found. I wonder about how much they will think of you and what you would have thought during their great plays.

I wish your two kids had been enough to keep you here. But like Pastor Terryl says, you were not in your right mind and couldn't even have considered the effect on your family. I still just can't seem to get my arms around that entire event – you killing yourself. So violent and desperate and, basically, insane.

Got to go.

March 27, 2008

Hi Howard.

Luke had his second scrimmage today and I went to see it. He is playing shortstop and is pretty darn good. He had a great play and *also had an excellent hit. He is so tall and handsome – his shoulders and chest are filling out and his voice is so deep. Often when people call here, they mistake him for you.*

*It was my first time sitting alone in the bleachers this year, and my first time watching my son play high school baseball. He is going to be wonderful, and I am so proud of him. I just wish so very much you were here to see him. And of course, to sit next to me. It's hard to fully enjoy the kids and all their accomplishments without you here.*

*I wish I knew a little more about how heaven works. People write in cards, "Howard is right beside you" but, quite frankly, I don't know if that's true. I mean, in heaven there are no tears or sadness or fear, so how could you possibly be right beside us? You would cry if you were because we are surrounded by sadness and despair, and there's no crying in heaven.*

*I don't know, Howard – I really thought so many times you had it in you to make it. That's why I stayed married to you for more than twenty years. We talked, probably more than a hundred times, about getting you better and happier. Maybe I just have to come to the conclusion that you suffered from mental illness, mainly severe depression, and in the end it was too much.*

*Maybe someday I will accept that and move on although I don't have much faith in that "moving on" philosophy. Basically, the way I see it is that I just learn to live with your suicide a little better each day. Some days I can live my life with some laughter, and then other days I just barely live my life.*

*If I actually sit and think on your suicide and the enormity of what has occurred and the overall effect on our lives, I could actually go crazy. I wouldn't be able to function. So I try not to think so deep into it – I just cannot.*

*What purpose would it serve to dwell on it, relive it constantly and meditate on the great loss and sadness? I don't think I could breathe or even move if I allowed myself to fall into such deep thoughts of what we have truly lost. What is done is done.*

*Got to go. It is getting late and the kids need to go to bed.*

April 01, 2008

*Hi Howard.*

*Just had a conversation with Meri O'Hara. We were talking about your death and the Memorial Day holiday. Memorial Day was the day you shot yourself.*

*I don't think we can be in the house that weekend this year.*

*Just the thought of you being home alone that whole day and us coming home to find you still alive with the head wound – just way too much to take. Thoughts of that day make my throat close and my chest get tight and, of course, my stomach turn. I can feel the stomach problem returning.*

*Oh God, I pray you help us through the next two months, please. Keep our minds clear and our thoughts only on good things.*

*Howard, I have an interview tomorrow for BOCES – a school nurse teacher position. Maybe Jesus can tell you about it. I am praying it is God's will and it works out. At least then I can work close to home, get a pension and even go get my Masters. Maybe even make a difference in some kid's life, who knows?*

*The kids are doing okay. I think the week of Easter coupled with your birthday that same week was a real emotional time for us all, and the kids were drained. This is so very hard, so sad. I wonder if the sadness ever goes away?*

*I hope and pray Trisha and Luke will be okay in the end – not too many hang-ups or problems with having a dad who committed suicide.*

*Got to go. Right now a thunderstorm is coming. You have no idea how much Trisha and I miss you when storms come – it's so comforting to have a man in the house when it is thundering and lightning.*

*Bye for now, Howie. Wish you were here, as always.*

*April 05, 2008*

Hi Howard.

I had some thoughts lately of all our times at the Jersey Shore. That was probably the one time each year (except for hunting) that you were most relaxed and happy. I loved watching you fish. I loved walking out to see you at the edge of the water. You always gave me a rough kiss on the cheek, and of course it hurt because you didn't shave while we were down there.

Spring is starting and so are the baseball and softball games. I sit there in the stands without you watching Luke play, with the knowledge that everyone around me knows you shot yourself. I know they wonder about you and me and the kids – about how we're doing and about why you, a father of two wonderful kids, did this to your family.

I have fear back again. I have no job, no lover and not much hope of either. And I am having trouble lately with God. I just don't feel Him, don't sense Him. Is He real?

I guess I'm still so depressed. Most days I stay busy and try to hide it. Luke and Trisha go about their days and try so hard to stay involved and enjoy life, but it is such an uphill battle. Often, I just want to give up, but I keep trying for Trisha and Luke. I know I haven't given my best. Most days, I'm happy to just get them up and out and get myself dressed. But I don't want to stay this way. I want to do better.

Part of me wants so badly to meet someone and fall in love again. I think I made an okay wife; would you agree, Howard? Certainly there are much hotter looking women around, but I am not too bad; would you agree, Howard? You and I just fit so well, and I doubt I can find that twice in one life.

Someone – some woman – told Diane that she would never be able to forgive her husband if he killed himself. I have thought the same thing myself at times. I am so mad at you. I often think of the selfishness involved in killing yourself, but I also know I could be very wrong on that point. I mean, I don't know how crazy you were.

How long did you battle severe depression? Anger? You were pretty depressed the entire time I knew you. You were often unable to enjoy anything. But really, even after twenty-three years with you, how well did I know you? And that is what scares me about meeting someone new. You never really know someone else, do you?

I've got to go. I'm tired, and thinking of you and typing to you is draining. There are no answers, so most of the time typing in this journal is discouraging.

Love, Me

April 08, 2008

Hi Howard.

Some thoughts for today.

I am re-arranging our – or should I say my – bedroom. My bedroom. I changed it right after you died, but I ended up putting it back the way it was. It was comforting that way. But you know what? To move on, I have to make some changes, so I thought I would start with the bedroom.

I still don't feel comfortable with the new arrangement, but I'm going to keep it this way. I hope and pray it will eventually grow on me and be the way my room is supposed to feel. I even splurged and bought a new headboard and footboard and two new bedside tables. As you know, I had to throw out our Ethan Allen headboard with your blood on it – I think it would have driven the dogs crazy always being able to smell you.

All this thought of moving on is difficult. People say moving on doesn't mean forgetting and doesn't mean giving up the person who died. But you know what? You do end up giving up some things – like the unrealistic, deep down thought that you just might come back. Seriously, by moving on and changing things, I have to face the cold fact that you are not coming back. That is such a difficult thing to do.

Each time I move on or the kids move on, we give up a part of you in our lives.

This baseball and softball season for Luke and Trisha are the very first without you. Their participation despite your absence is, in fact, moving on. They are making memories that do not include you; hence, the loss is big.

I thought of something earlier when I was bringing the garbage out – you moved on. I'm right, aren't I? You have moved on, so I guess we need to do the same. We can't stay stuck here forever although it's all we have known for the last ten months.

So I was thinking, the kids and I need to find a way to move on so that we also can continue to have you in our lives. I'm going to see if they would like to start a scrap book or something to start capturing memories. I'm also thinking that maybe I could send a letter to some of your old friends to see if they have a story or two or a picture they could send us. Perhaps then we can start putting together some type of memory book.

I thought of you the other night. What were you doing up in heaven? Were you walking along with Jesus? What were you discussing? Do you see us? Do you smile at seeing us? Do you know us?

Got to go. The dogs want some company. Diesel has become my "boyfriend." He's always wanting to be next to me and get attention. He is such a gentleman. I can tell he must long for you and think about you.

You broke his heart, do you know that?

*April 2008*

## Spaces

*It's the empty spaces*
*The vacant shed*
*The quiet basement*
*The unused tools*
*The web-filled corners*
*The idle fishing poles*
*The unworn clothes*
*The silent motors*
*The untouched coins*

*It's these empty spaces*
*that make little cuts*
*In what used to be my spirit*
*Do these scars heal?*

*April 14, 2008*

Hi Howard.

I just was thinking of how you were my best friend, you know that? I know I have many close girlfriends, especially from childhood. But I was never one of those women who would say I had a girlfriend closer to me than my husband. You were the one person I could say anything to, as you would never repeat it! Isn't that weird?

I lost so much when I lost you – my best friend, my lover, my husband, my house mate, my protector (that's a scary one to lose), the father of my children, dog walker, house repairman, car repairman, financial supporter, bug killer, drain unclogger ...

I feel very lost and without a firm foundation right now. I truly don't know which way to turn and it's been almost eleven months since you died. I just cannot seem to get it together, Howard. Do I clean? Pay the bills? Wash clothes? Walk the dogs? Look for a job?

I am tired, Howard. Tired of being sad, depressed, confused, sluggish, lazy and immobile. I pray my life starts getting itself together.

Trisha and Luke are forever wounded and changed by your death, Howard. I have no idea if they will make it or not.

Love you, Howard

Your wife

April 24, 2008

Hi Howard.

Well, we're back from our Florida trip. I think I won't be taking another trip to Florida for a long time. It was just too painful going there without you.

I guess my brother Jimmy is right – we need to make new memories. But it is so hard because in every situation since you died, I am with family and the same people you and I were always with. All that's missing is you. Your absence is glaring.

So let me see. I imagine we need to make memories with some other people who weren't such a big part of our lives when you were alive. But that means getting to know new people.

The kids will have an easier time at that because being in high school is really all about making memories – and they were never in high school while you were alive. So basically, all their high school memories will be new ones without the constant reminder of you suddenly not being there. Does any of this make any sense at all?

I missed you so very much while in Florida, especially when I was in the pool. I used to love swimming with you and climbing on your back, and you would float around with me hanging onto you –

most likely, that was the only place you could really hold me up. Anyway, I missed kissing the top of your head. Usually in the pool was the only time I ever saw the top of your head, you were so tall.

How are you, Howard? So many guys miss you – Frank Shanley, Steve O, Mark Warren. I saw each of them this week, and they all said they think of you every day. Steve told me that he just says to himself, why Howard? And he just shakes his head.

I have been keeping in touch with John, which you already know being that you're in heaven. He's quite funny and talks up a storm – I think I have talked to him more in the last six months than I spoke to you in ten years. I am not comparing – you are different people – but it's nice to chat with someone who talks more than I do. I love listening to his stories.

So Howard, what do you think? You know me better than anyone and you know darn well I would be lousy at dating other men. Did you perhaps send John to me? He is a great deal like you in many ways, such as his love for hunting and the outdoors.

Howard, can you say a prayer to Jesus that whoever ends up in my life comes soon and comes without baggage? Someone who has values and will be with me forever with no games or hurtful actions? I just couldn't live through that, so please pray for me and the kids about this, okay? Thanks.

Got to go. Remember I used to call you Tub sometimes? Boy, Tub, I could sure go for one of your hugs right now!

Love you forever.
Your wife

*Trisha, Trish, Luke and Grandma on the Florida trip eleven months after Howard's suicide*

*April 25, 2008*

*Spring was the last season you were alive*
*And with us here*
*I remember you walking into the backyard*
*Remember seeing you with the cigar in your mouth*
*Your baggy jeans hanging in the back*
*Dirt on your hands and face*
*The slow way you walked, slightly bent over*
*Your skin already tan in May*
*I remember how you smelled*
*How you talked*
*Always looking for things to do*
*Something to fix or clean up*
*We would work on our yard together*
*You and I*
*How I loved springtime with you*
*It was always the first time in many months*
*We would be outside together*
*Sometimes holding hands*
*I loved our talks on the front steps as the nights grew warmer*
*Just as the sun would go down we would stop*
*Both of us taking seats on the front steps*
*Usually with Diesel lying right in front of our feet*
*We would talk about baseball, flowers, mulch*
*Discuss Luke and Trisha, maybe even your back*
*How you were doing, how my work was going*
*Vacation plans would be tossed about*
*No matter the topic*
*Each of those quiet times on the steps were hopeful*
*Full of plans, satisfaction in a day's work done*
*I felt young and content with you on those nights*
*No thought of losing you or me*
*No fear or despair or sadness*

Just a relaxed time together with the fresh smell of flowers
Birds nearby, some singing, some settling down
We would wave to a neighbor or two
After a bit you would get up to close the shed or gate
I would pick up a few things and get the kids together
We would all go inside for the night
At peace, rested and wrapped warm in each other's presence
They are the last memories I have of you
Memories of you in springtime
I didn't know that last springtime didn't bring you hope
Why did I miss your slower pace?
Your back bent further down?
Why did I miss the sadness in your eyes?
Was I too busy greeting spring to notice you?
I don't know if we sat outside together last May
Now we won't ever again
Spring is full of hope and brightness and warmth
Our springtime now brings sadness and longing
Longing for you and our talks on the steps
Your smell, your walk, your baggy pants
How I miss you, Howard
I close the shed and the gate now with a heavy heart
Wishing beyond all wishes that I could have you here again
I don't want this spring to end
For when it ends so do my last memories of you, Howard
Spring was the last season we had you, Howard
How I miss you

*April 30, 2008*

Why is it so hard to let go of the past? I feel as if we – the three of us – are clinging to the side of a big ship, dangling way above the ocean waters, and God is asking us to open our hands and let go.

*The ship is moving very fast, and He says to just let go. Let go of the past and the hurts.*

*That means letting go of you, Howard, and I just don't think I can do that. People say, "That's what Howard would want you to do – let go and move on." Quite honestly, I don't care what you would want, Howard! You are in heaven, peaceful, joyful and sharing life with Jesus. We are down here, fearful, anxious and in pain. What you would want for us doesn't count.*

*God, how do we let go of that ship's railing, let go of Howard, and move on? What if what lies ahead holds even more anguish and sadness? Why would I want to let go of the pain and sorrow I already have just to experience more? At least I know what I've got!*

*Taking chances with new people is just too scary. People disappoint. I know that because I have been a disappointment to others, so why would I take a chance on anyone else? How do you take a chance on letting go without losing your own life and spirit? I can't handle any more disappointment, God, and neither can the kids.*

*God, you will have to open one or two doors before I move on. Please! I don't think that is a lot to ask. I've been looking for you for the past year now. I cannot feel you. I don't sense your presence. Why is it so hard for you to send one sign? Open one door? Please.*

*May 04, 2008*

*Hi Howard.*

*Went by to see you today at the cemetery. I know you're not there, but it's easier to talk to you and Jesus there. It was beautiful – the smells of spring along with some cool sounds that you only hear this time of year.*

*I was thinking of you after your last surgery, when you were still a little high from the anesthesia. You were so damn sweet – telling* me you really loved me and asking me if I knew that. Holding my hand while you were telling me. Damn, it was so nice.

This grief stuff is so sharp and even violent sometimes in how it arrives. I cannot plan for it, and I almost can never control it. The only thing that helps me some days is humor – me being funny or someone near me who has a sense of humor. Definitely a good thing to have one or two people around with a sense of humor, but that isn't always easy. Not many people smiling these days, you know?

The issue of men is going to come up soon, Howard, and I don't want to go there. I hate wanting to be with someone else. I don't want to have to date or get to know someone else. I am not a good dater – never was. You were the only one I dated and then I married you, so what does that tell you?

I need to learn to move forward and live a new life. I've been trying to put the old one back together again, but that's not working. The puzzle pieces have been completely scattered. The box dropped and all one thousand pieces fell out, and I've been trying in vain to put them together into some formation that resembles the picture on the front of the box. It's not working.

Here's a poem.

*The pieces of the puzzle can fall by the side*
*Lie on the floor*
*Settle under the chair*
*They make their way under the rug*
*You work on this puzzle*
*Never knowing pieces are missing*
*You can't understand sometimes why something isn't fitting*
*Then you come across a piece or two*
*While doing everyday things*

*You wonder*
*Just how many more am I missing?*
*Are these the ones that really belong*

*To the puzzle I'm doing?*
*They could very well belong to another puzzle*
*You can bend the edges*
*Twist the pieces to fit*
*Never sits right after that*
*Always bent and never lying flat*

*You just don't want to remove those pieces though*
*You're not sure you will ever find the right ones that fit*
*You figure you can settle for almost fitting*
*Then one pops up and out*
*Leaves a hole*
*Something needs to fill it*
*Usually dirt and dust*
*Nothing you can look at*
*and admire*

*May 22, 2008*

Hi Howard.

Finally, after eleven months and twenty-four days, I looked at the CD my brother made of our pictures and put to music. It's pictures of you with all of us throughout the twenty-three years I was with you. This is the first time I've looked at it.

I don't know what to say. What happened?! You can tell by the pictures that you and I were meant to be.

Boy, did I have a lot of different hair colors! Howard, you were so handsome and so full of promise and talent. How did things go from those pictures – us, you and me, Luke and Trisha – to you shooting yourself? How could the kids and I not be enough to make you stay around? I will never get it this side of heaven. May God grant me some answers when I get to where you are.

Howard, I love you. Always have and always will.

*God, please tell Howard that for me, and let him know I will never love another like him. By looking at these pictures, God, you can see Howard was loved by me and my family, that is for sure.*

*I hope that was enough while you were here, Howard. I tried.*

May 30, 2008<br>One Year Anniversary of Howard's Death

*Dear God,*

*Just a month ago, I wrote to you, God, asking why you couldn't open just one door for us.*

*Well, today, one month later and exactly on the year anniversary of Howard's death, I received a call from BOCES about the school nurse teacher job I interviewed for the other day. And they say I have the position!*

*First, thank you, God.*

*Second, please forgive my constant doubts.*

*Third, I get such a kick out of how you work and the times we get to see you work, Lord!*

*Fourth, it's a sign for us to take a few steps towards moving on, God. I cannot let go of the railing just yet, but I am close.*

*Fifth, don't be mad, but I asked for one or two signs and the compensation court hearings are this week, God, on Thursday and Friday, so you could always work the second sign through having those events go our way!*

*I know you know, God, what I am thinking right now – no matter how many signs I ask you for, I will never think it is enough, will I? I'll keep coming back to you asking for more reassurance that you are real, you love us and you are in control.*

*I am much closer to seeing and believing that than I have ever been, God. Please just have patience with me and how I usually don't get it right. At least I'm on the right path for now, God!*

*Thanks, God, for loving us!*

# 13

## Keep Calm, Eat Bacon and Believe in the Bear

I have always been fascinated by the reports of others who claim some kind of connection with or message from a dead loved one or God Himself.

Before Howard died, I had only had one episode I would consider otherworldly. I think of it now in terms of a slogan on a T-shirt I once gave to Trisha: *Keep Calm and Eat Bacon.*

We were living on Montgomery Street in Goshen, and the kids were toddlers. Howard and I were working opposite shifts – he worked nights, I worked days.

One night, I was awakened from a dead sleep at about two a.m. by the smell of bacon. It was overwhelming, like someone was cooking a full pound of bacon at once. I figured Howard was home and hungry, and he was cooking up some bacon. But why would he do that at this hour, when he should have known the smell would disturb my sleep?

I lay there for a bit listening for noise from the kitchen downstairs, but I soon realized it was completely silent in the house. Weird. I decided to check.

I quietly got up and headed to the hallway. The kitchen light was on, just as I'd left it when I went to bed. I leaned over the railing and listened. I heard no footsteps, no cooking noises, no sound of sizzling bacon.

But the smell was very pervasive. It seemed to surround me rather than emanate from one location.

"Howard?" I said.

No answer.

I walked partway down the staircase.

"Howard?" I said again, a little louder this time.

Once again, no answer.

Finally, I walked all the way down, through the front hallway and the living room and on into the kitchen.

The room was empty. There was no frying pan, no bacon, no Howard. The kitchen was just as I'd left it when I went to bed.

I had only one certain thought: "My God, Howard is dead and this is his way of telling me!"

Well, it seemed to make sense at the time. Howard loved bacon, no question, but I couldn't imagine why he'd cook up some bacon in the third dimension during a last-minute visit to me on his way up to heaven. Still, I was sure he was dead and the bacon was his way of letting me know.

I was actually very upset. I went back up to my bed to wait for the phone to ring and give me the news that I already knew. I lay there for close to two hours waiting as the bacon smell slowly dissipated. Part of my mind kept wondering, where did it *come* from while the other part of me was sure that my dead husband had sent it.

Howard came home at the end of his shift, as usual. I told him I was very glad to see him because I was sure he'd died on the road and had sent me the smell of his favorite food as a final farewell. There was no lingering scent of bacon in the house to help prove my point.

* * *

My next experience with the other side occurred the day after Howard died, and it had to do with an orchid.

I had purchased the orchid about three years earlier, and its beautiful pinkish purple color had caught my eye. But I had the worst luck nurturing that orchid. It grew outwards instead of upwards. And it bloomed only about twice a year. When it did, it produced only one lonesome bud.

The single bud would appear, open up, be beautiful, then fall off and die.

About two weeks before Howard died, I called my sister-in-law Diane and asked her what she thought I should do about it. She gave me her best advice about what kind of soil I should buy and how to repot it without killing it. That evening, I remember telling Howard I was going to repot the orchid and give it a better chance of flourishing.

I figured he was barely listening to me and expected him to say something vague like "Okay." But he didn't. Instead, he seemed angry about it.

"Why don't you just leave it alone?" he said. "Why do you have to mess with it? Just leave it alone."

I told him it might help the plant thrive if I gave it a new pot and soil to grow in, but Howard was determined that I shouldn't.

"Just leave it alone!" he repeated.

I remember saying, "Jeez, whatever, okay, I'll leave it alone," and then walking away.

I didn't look at that orchid again until the day after Howard shot himself. It was Tuesday night, about twenty-four hours after I'd found him. I was standing at the kitchen sink looking out the bay window when I noticed the orchid on the window sill. It was sticking straight out to the right as it always did, but this time it had eight – yes, *eight* – buds on it.

There's no way, I thought. Then I counted them again – one, two, three, four, five, six, seven and eight.

My goodness, I thought. Was God speaking to me – or was Howard?

But then, on second thought, I figured it wasn't actually a sign from God. If it were, it would have seven buds, not eight. Seven is a very important number in the Bible. "Too bad it's not seven," I thought. (I like to think it was the shock I was in that caused me to have this weirdly negative reaction.)

For the first time in its life, though, that orchid was actually stunning. For the next seven days, a new bud opened up. One a day.

The Tuesday of the seventh bloom was the day we buried Howard.

I woke the day after the funeral expecting to see the eighth and final bud open and blooming when I went down to the kitchen. But do you know what? That eighth bud – the one that made me think it couldn't be a sign from God – well, that eighth bud was lying on the windowsill, unopened. It had fallen off the stem during the night.

It never bloomed.

I don't know. Perhaps God was telling me it would be okay. Or maybe it was a message from Howard, who'd had such strong feelings about leaving the orchid alone. I just don't know.

The orchid lived one more year after that. It never produced another bud again. It died never having blossomed again.

A part of me held onto the hope of those seven blossoms, but another part of me regretted ever seeing its beauty because then it died. It was gone, just like Howard.

\*\*\*

And then there is the bear.

About ten years before Howard killed himself, he made a wood carving for me. It was his rendition of our walk through life together, and it still hangs on my wall. Why bears? Who knows. It was what Howard chose to represent us.

*Howard's bear carving*

Bears are quite scarce in our region. I know there are some living in nearby wooded areas, but they largely keep themselves hidden. I think, more than anything, they're scared of humans.

Certainly, there's never been a bear sighted anywhere near Grace Community Church in Washingtonville, where Howard's funeral was held. The church is surrounded by a large parking lot, and there are houses on either side of the church property. A busy road, Route 94, runs in front of the church. Behind it, well back from the parking lot, is a wooded area.

Pastor Terryl, who has been at the church since its founding more than twenty years ago and who officiated at Howard's funeral, will tell you that he never once saw a bear in all those years. Not at night, not at dusk and certainly not in the middle of the day.

But on the morning of June 4, 2007, when more than one hundred people filed into Grace Community for Howard Nelson's funeral service, a brown bear could be seen slowly walking the perimeter of the church property. It was reported that he stayed away from everyone, but that he walked along the property line as if he wanted to be a part of the event but keep his distance at the same time.

Many people saw the bear. I did not. I was told about the bear at the reception after the burial. I thought to myself, yes, that makes sense. That could have been Howard. I tucked the incident away. But not for long.

The day after the funeral, I took a ride to Howard's grave alone. Slate Hill Cemetery is a beautiful, old burial ground with grave markers dating back to the 1800s. Howard is in the newer section, not too far back. You drive in a little ways, then make a right, then a sharp left. He's there, on your right-hand side.

I parked directly in front of Howard's fresh grave. There was the large mound of dirt on top with some flower arrangements placed around it. The grave marker with Howard's name on it had been set in place by the funeral home.

I made my way toward the grave marker, prepared to be overwhelmed with fresh grief at seeing my husband's name, date of birth and date of death all permanently etched into the metal plate. As I walked toward it, I noticed a very large, brown moist mound of something directly in front of it.

"You've got to be kidding me!" I thought. But there was no doubt what it was. Directly in front of Howard's grave marker was a very large pile of bear poop. Bear poop, okay? Not deer pellets or bird droppings or dog poop.

It was bear poop.

Some bear had made his way out of the woods at the far side of the cemetery, lumbered past dozens and dozens of headstones and graves in order to ceremoniously poop right on Howard's grave.

I felt a mix of anger, surprise and utter disbelief.

"Well, Howard, thanks for the awesome gift!" I said out loud. "But listen, if you plan to leave any more mementos for the kids and me, a pile of money would actually be far more useful than a pile of poop."

Over the next few years, the visiting bear showed up now and then, both live and in art form. I have heard that sometimes departed loved ones visit in animal form, so I am guessing Howard chose the form of a bear. Perhaps he could relate to its size – Howard was a big man. Or perhaps it was the way the bear moved – slowly, deliberately and with purpose, yet fast when it came to protecting his territory or family. If you have ever observed a bear, you probably noted that there was no rushing, no hysterics.

I received two gifts involving bears that summer of 2007. One was a set of four brown bear statues, each a different size and pose. The other was a statue of a bear holding a lantern. It was intended to be displayed outdoors with a candle in the lantern, as though the bear was a night watchman guarding our family.

Neither of the gift givers knew of the bear sighting at the funeral.

In June 2007 I noticed what once again looked like bear poop, this time in the backyard. Mind you, we live in a high traffic area right off Fletcher Street. This is not exactly the middle of the woods.

But it seems that Howard as a bear was attracted to a beautiful mulberry tree in the yard, right next to the above-ground pool. For about a month every summer, the tree has large purple berries on it. When the birds eat the berries, of course, they expel purple poop all over the neighborhood.

And that summer, we had a bear climb the chain-link fence and apparently eat berries off the tree. Our evidence?

First of all, Diesel went mad barking at something in the back yard in the middle of the night. (He'd long since quit barking at deer, so this was unusual.)

Second, there was a large area of matted grass just beneath the tree.

Third, I found a large mound of bear poop just under the tree. Again with the poop! I'm going to have to ask Howard about this when I see him in heaven! The fathers in the neighborhood didn't believe it was bear poop until one of them brought a sample to the local police, who verified that this widow lady wasn't crazy. It was, in fact, bear poop.

And fourth, I found a major indentation on our metal fence, most likely made when the bear hit the fence full force running from the madly barking Diesel.

Over the next few years, the bear visited our yard regularly, most especially when the berries were ripe for eating.

But the bear visits also seemed to coincide with events surrounding Luke.

We had frequent visits from the bear during the year Luke was a high school senior, when he earned his Eagle Scout rank, went to his first prom and graduated.

The one time I saw the bear myself was on the night of Luke's graduation party in our back yard. The party went on and on. Finally, at 3:30 a.m., I told Luke's friends for the last time, "The party's over!"

About an hour later, after we all finally turned in, we had a visitor to our backyard, apparently interested in the party leftovers. Diesel stood at the back porch door making a very low guttural growl – a noise he made only when he perceived *extreme* danger.

I stood behind Diesel. I was unable to see what the danger was, but I knew instinctively that it was the bear. I slowly opened the sliding glass door fervently hoping the bear wasn't on the porch. Daisy, my brave (but not so bright) girl, immediately threw herself out the door to give chase to whatever was there. Diesel, the smarter and more cowardly of the two, stayed planted in the doorway. If Daisy wanted to be the heroine, fine with him.

As I stepped out the door I heard it. The bear was *under* me, directly under the porch. In a flash, he ran out on all fours faster than I ever imagined a bear could run. I saw his back end and, within seconds, he was across the yard. With a loud bang he hit the fence, and was quickly over it and onto Craig's lawn.

That was June 2011 – Luke's graduation night and the last summer before he left for college. We never saw or heard the bear again.

The berry tree remains there and in full bloom. Only the birds now partake of the sweet treats it produces each summer.

\* \* \*

It also appears that either Howard or perhaps some other departed relative began visiting us in the form of an eagle.

No lie.

It was spring 2009 and I was outside, in front of the house. The blue sky was gorgeous. I looked up – I've looked up more in the last six years than I had in my entire lifetime before Howard died – and way up high, I saw two bald eagles. At least that's what I thought they were. Eagles are a rarity in our sky and I wondered, could it possibly be?

I ran in to get binoculars. When I got back out front, they were even higher in the sky. But I could tell through the binoculars that these were the real thing – white tails and white heads and, my goodness, their wing span was enormous! They were beautiful – two eagles flying together over the Village of Goshen. Amazing.

No one else was outside to see them and verify that they were, indeed, eagles. I had to hope they would return.

I saw them again about a week later. I was driving home and had made a left onto Fletcher Street. Just as I hit the top of the hill, I was granted the privilege of seeing one of those beautiful birds, now even closer. He was sitting high up on a branch of an old, nearly dead tree. He was stunning and so majestic.

I stopped and got out of the car with my phone camera. As I approached the bottom of the tree, the bird looked down. No rush, no move to take off. He just stared at me as I took the picture. My lousy phone camera doesn't do him justice.

When I told people about it, some would say, "Oh that's Howard coming to visit and watch over you all."

Probably not. He was busy visiting and pooping as a bear, but it was awesome nonetheless.

That fall, about four months after my eagle sightings, I was on one of my many four-mile walks that started (or ended) on Fletcher Street. I was walking up the steep hill and, as I hit the crest, there he was – the eagle again!

This time he flew directly above me toward the village. The *village!* He flew effortlessly and was soon too far and too high to see.

The eagles flew by several times that fall, and a few of my neighbors were outside to see them – at last, I wasn't the only one. We were blessed enough to have more sightings of them during the following spring and fall of 2010 as well as 2011. Sometimes there was one, sometimes two soaring silently from one end of the village to the other.

But it is my final encounter with the eagles that stands out in my memory.

I had met a woman who was, apparently, a card reader. We got talking and the conversation turned to Howard and his death. She took a moment to ponder and then, seemingly out of the blue, she asked me if I knew that Howard comes to me as an eagle.

Wow, pretty good! I laughed and told her some of my eagle stories. She didn't laugh with me. She just said yes, that's him. She said he was around us and was perhaps blocking the next person who was to come into my life.

On that same day, Trisha told me that she'd had this overwhelming urge to talk to her father. She felt the need to ask him to please leave Mommy alone now – that he was smothering me and he needed to give me room to move on.

Trisha also knew that if she ever needed her father all she had to do was call to him.

I came home that afternoon and told Trisha about my conversation with the woman who asked if I knew that Daddy was coming to me as an eagle.

Trisha said, "I have to tell you something, Mom."

Oh goodness, what now?

Trisha told me about her urge to ask her father to leave me alone. We talked a bit about this, and we marveled over the fact that, yes, we had seen quite a number of eagles and – who knows? – perhaps it was him.

Then I walked out the front door. I looked up and there, hovering over the trees near the Quinns' house, was a bald eagle. I watched as he flew away. I saw only the side of his head, his awesome wing span and his beautiful white tail.

I have never seen another eagle since that day.

It took me five years to make the connection, but one day it finally hit me. The largest etching on Howard's headstone is an eagle – a majestic beautiful eagle designed by Trisha herself and etched by an artist in Vermont.

He'd been there all along. It just took me a while to realize it.

\* \* \*

Of the three of us, Trisha has had the most dreams and visions of Howard. Her first dream occurred when Howard was being waked.

Trisha was elated as she talked about this dream. She was in the shed where there was (in her dream) a large, broken, dirty, dingy used fish tank. Trisha said it was filthy and the glass was broken, with moss and mold growing on it. It had no life.

Howard came to Trisha in this dream outside of the shed. When Trisha told this part, her eyes lit up. She looked far off and smiled. She talked about how Howard walked toward her in the dream, strong like she remembered him; a solid man with a determined step.

She said his smile was amazing. He himself was all light and shine. She said there was a glow about him and beautiful light around him. He was so very happy, Trisha said. So happy and smiling and at ease. Howard told Trisha he was okay, that she would be okay, too.

Then Trisha went back into the shed, and the fish tank was suddenly so beautiful. It was filled with colorful fish and with bright, shining light. The water was clean and lovely. It was all new and full of life.

To Trisha and to Luke and me, her dream meant Howard's life was now beautiful. He was alive, free of pain and reborn. He was okay, and we would be, too.

\* \* \*

Two Bible verses have come to mean a great deal to the kids and me. It seemed that they gained significance in our lives by accident, but we are all quite sure now that it was by design.

Howard received the gift of a Bible about ten years before he died, when he was in rehab. There are a few notations written on various pages in that Bible.

The Bible is hard cover and the inside of the back cover is dark blue, nearly black. If anyone were to write on that particular page, it would be nearly impossible to make out the words.

After Howard died, the kids and I chose Matthew 28:20 to appear on the cake served following the funeral: "Lo, I am with you always, even unto the end of the age." We don't remember why we chose this verse; I just remember it affecting the three of us deeply after his death.

We also chose that verse to be written just below the eagle on Howard's headstone. It is beautiful.

Just before my breakdown that first year, I came upon another short Bible verse that I clung to for dear life: "Be Not Afraid."

Six months later, I was looking through Howard's Bible. I turned to that dark inside page of the back cover, and suddenly I saw clearly that it had writing on it I had never seen before.

It was in Howard's handwriting and it said, "Lo, I am with you always, even unto the end of the age."

I have no idea when Howard wrote that. Maybe it was ten years before he died, maybe it was the day he died. But he wrote it, and we had chosen it to comfort us after he was gone.

I looked further and found it. He had also underlined the three words that I so desperately wanted to live by: "Be Not Afraid."

Clearly, I needed to look at more than bear poop in order to find Howard.

# 14

# Diesel and Daisy

I never anticipated how much attention two traumatized dogs would need, but I found out fast once Howard was dead.

During the two years before Howard died, he was home most of the time, so doggie detail had fallen pretty much to him. Howard was their primary caretaker and entertainment, and both dogs worshipped him, especially Diesel.

But it was all on me after Howard was gone. Suddenly, I was the center of two dogs' lives, and I had to learn how to take care of them along with a few hundred other things I was suddenly in charge of.

I was also in charge of trying to help those poor dogs through their own grief. They nearly curled up and died after Howard was gone.

Diesel was born July 4, 2005, shortly after we put Chili down. I was at the Goshen farmers market one day telling the specialty dog food lady about Chili's sad ending, and she promptly told me she thought she knew of a puppy for us. A golden retriever breeder on Sarah Wells Trail still had one unclaimed male because the original buyer never showed up with a deposit.

Of course I flew right down there to see the litter. The puppies were an unbelievably pure, gorgeous white. The pup who would become ours was the one sleeping like a lump behind the food bowl. I would've taken out a second mortgage to have him, but it turned out he cost only as much as a good used car. A lot, I admit, but did I care?

The breeder had to check out my references and would get back to me. I gave her a deposit and headed home to tell Howard how much money we were about to spend on a dog. We brought him home the next week.

I named him Diesel, but he earned a nickname almost immediately. We started calling him Whiz, largely because the kids and I were astonished by how often he needed to take one. I swear, he peed a minimum of twenty times on every walk.

Trisha eventually gave him a second nickname. Handsome Man. He is, and he knows it. He truly does.

Diesel was Howard's dog right from the start. He rode in that diesel Ford pick-up truck of Howard's, and he fit right in. There was Howard, behind the wheel wearing his Chicago Bears hat, cigar in mouth.

And his passenger? It was always Diesel, sitting ramrod straight, eyes forward. No sudden movements for this dog. Nope, he moved just like his owner – SLOWLY. When he looked to the left, he turned slowly to the left. When he looked to the right, he turned slowly to the right. He might lean toward the window a bit for an admirer to pet him, but mostly he sat quietly and waited for his gushing fan to come to him.

That dog loved Howard's truck, and he spent so much time in it with Howard during their twenty-two months together that they became known around town as quite a couple. They were inseparable at home, too. When Howard walked to the back yard, Diesel followed. When Howard worked in the front yard or on the cars, Diesel was there. I still find it hard to believe that Howard chose to kill himself and leave this dog behind.

In November 2006, about seven months before Howard died, we adopted Daisy Mae, a small, black mixed breed who had been abandoned on the side of the road when she was a two-pound puppy. The woman who found her said the pup wasn't moving much, and she didn't think she'd live. That wonderful good Samaritan brought the puppy to a veterinarian at PetSmart in Middletown, which is where we got involved.

Trisha went nuts when we saw her sitting in the woman's lap waiting her turn with the vet. Ooooh, can we have her, Trisha wanted to know. I told the woman that if the puppy lived, give me a call. She did, and the rest is history.

We named her Daisy Mae, but she got nicknamed right away, too – Fizz, of course. Fizz and Whiz. And Crazy Daisy, what else?

Daisy found life a very serious business right from the start. Lots of protecting, monitoring and surveying. She found Diesel's laid back demeanor both confusing and contemptible. She thought Diesel was so damn lame, sometimes. For his part, Diesel was completely unimpressed and wanted nothing to do with her.

He snubbed her.

As soon as she was grown a bit, though, Daisy took charge of Diesel. One of her first self-appointed jobs was to teach him some manners. Diesel liked to jump up on visitors, and as soon as she was able, Daisy made him stop by jumping up on *his* back. She was seventy pounds lighter, but clearly she was the boss.

Still, they looked out for each other. Still do. When Daisy cries at the groomer (she is very melodramatic), Diesel frets because of it. And they bicker like sister and brother. You can tell when Daisy gets really pissed at Diesel, and do you know? He runs off looking over his shoulder at her, and I can almost see him laugh.

Daisy Mae quickly joined the Howard Nelson Admiration Society. Now it was Howard, Diesel and Daisy together all day. Diesel never gave up the passenger seat to Daisy but she didn't mind the back. And it was still just Diesel who accompanied Howard on his evening walks on the unpaved portion of the Heritage Trail, the rail trail that runs through Goshen.

I have learned since from Trisha that Howard always carried a switchblade with him on these walks. I find this interesting. Why did he think he needed to carry a weapon? And if he thought he needed one, why didn't he suggest I carry one when I went out walking?

After Howard's death, I had to give up that route with Diesel. For some reason, the dog always grew agitated when we hit a certain part of the route, and I was afraid he'd knock me to the ground with his hard pulling at the leash.

Just one more mystery.

*Daisy, front, and Diesel*

\* \* \*

One of my most vivid memories of the day Howard killed himself is the image of the dogs standing behind the child gate downstairs, wagging their tails so grateful to see the kids and me come into the house.

When I saw them down there, my first thought was, "This is not normal, the dogs locked down there when Howard is home." It just never happened. That image of the dogs, along with the wet snoring sounds I heard coming from upstairs, were what made me take the steps to the bedroom two at a time.

I didn't see the dogs again from that moment until about three days later. Our dog sitter Mona took them to her house although I don't remember calling her to come get them.

When we all finally did return to the house and the dogs came home from Mona's, I was shocked that neither of them went into my bedroom. I thought for sure they would make a beeline for the room looking for Howard or, at the very least, to smell the room. They didn't.

For the most part, they stayed downstairs or outside. They also slept in the hallway outside the bedroom, which stunned me. They had always slept in the crate next to our bed, but that was over.

To see Diesel slump down at the top of the stairs with his eyes downcast and his head on his paws broke my heart. I could hear him sigh out there in the hallway. Diesel is a sigher, and he was sighing his heartbreak.

Clearly, he was deeply depressed.

Daisy didn't suffer the same depression that Diesel did, but we would quickly come to find out that she had been traumatized by the sound of the gun shot. To this day, she has a panic attack whenever she hears a sudden loud noise. If a balloon pops or someone pops those packing bubbles, this poor puppy begins to violently shake and runs looking for a hiding spot.

But Diesel. He lay at the top of those stairs for three months. He wouldn't eat, he didn't want to walk, he had very little interaction with the kids or me. His sad eyes and lack of life began to seriously worry me.

I took him to the vet about three weeks after the funeral. "Please tell me he isn't going to be like this forever," I told the vet. "I can't stand his sadness."

The vet said Diesel was mourning, just like the rest of us. And yes, he would eventually come out of it. He predicted that Diesel would one day simply turn his allegiance and love totally onto me as if a light switch had clicked on.

We looked at his sad face all that June, July and August. Then, one night at the beginning of September, it happened just as the vet said it would.

Diesel and Daisy had never slept in our bed. There simply wasn't any room. But that September night I remember waking up thinking, "Someone is in bed with me."

I reached over and felt ... fur. Mr. Diesel had quietly climbed up and lay down next to me. Not at the bottom of the bed but right *next* to me with his head on the pillow beside me. I was thrilled. (Little did I guess that, five years later, this wouldn't be so thrilling anymore.) But there he was.

In the morning, Daisy woke up and came looking for him. Diesel raised his head from the pillow and looked down at her as if to say, "Sorry, I got here first, and I'm not moving."

Daisy, of course, began whining (Did I mention that she's melodramatic?). She needed a boost up. I was so thrilled that Diesel was out of his mourning, that I helped Daisy up to join us.

That was my second mistake.

From that day forward, though, Diesel turned it around. He started eating – he had lost ten pounds that summer – and he started playing. He began to enjoy our walks every night and, little by little, he acted as if he were my one and only honey.

I once saw a T-shirt that said, "I sleep with dogs," and I think they had Diesel and me in mind when they developed that one.

What did linger was Diesel's yearning to be riding in the passenger seat of a diesel pick-up truck. For the first two years after Howard died, I dreaded the sound of a truck coming within earshot. Diesel would wake from a dead sleep at the sound. His ears would perk up, his eyes would light up and he would go running to the door.

You could almost feel the excitement and hope well up within him as he heard the sound of the diesel motor. It just set off some kind of hope in him and, being a dog, he didn't try to hide or disguise it. He just went with it – the hope and then the disappointment. And I would cry as he dropped his head to his paws again with a sigh.

\* \* \*

The dogs and I had a lot learn together about taking proper walks. Diesel was a puller, and he generally dragged me along behind him. And as small as she was, Daisy's tugging at the leash sometimes felt she was pulling my arm out of the socket.

One evening, I decided to take them to the duck pond two blocks down on Spring Street. I figured it would be nice for them to sniff the water, a change from our usual route down the other way by the Fletcher Street apartments. They became a bit excited about the new and interesting smells. Plus there was goose poop down there. How exciting!

At first, everyone did well. I had one dog on one side of me and one on the other. But then Diesel saw the geese in the water and the game was on. He yanked me forward. I landed on one knee, squarely mired in green goose poop. He hauled me to the edge of the pond, his whole body vibrating with excitement.

I expected him to jump into the water but Diesel, at heart, is a coward. He loved *looking* at the water, but anything in it that moved caused him to leap backwards. I threw a few small rocks into the water just to see him do it. He was totally bewildered and a bit of a scairdy ... dog.

But soon I was trapped in a tug of war – both dogs began to pull as hard as they could toward the water. They had made up their minds to go swimming. I tried to get close to the edge so they could get their feet wet. Of course, *that* wasn't going to be the end of it. Before long I found myself ankle deep in green water with lilies all around me.

It was at this point that the geese, probably concerned about their babies, started swimming *toward* us. They made no noise, just slowly progressed toward the crazy lady and her two wild animals. Eventually, we all got the message and high-tailed it out of there.

Clearly, I had to find a way to walk two dogs and carry a poop bag without being yanked all over town or into slimy, green water. We needed some ground rules – mine, not theirs.

I decided to get rid of their collars and switch to a pricey contraption called Gentle Leader. It goes around the muzzle but doesn't restrict the dog from opening his mouth or barking.

I tried putting it on Diesel first. I had to sit on him to get it on. As soon as I did, he began pawing at it to get rid of it. He looked like he was wiping his nose. I ignored his annoyance and headed out to walk him. We made it just past Craig and Sara's house next door when Diesel managed to get the thing off his nose.

Daisy witnessed the whole ordeal, and she decided she was having none of it. I never managed to get it on her.

My next purchase was a harness for the big guy. This got strapped to his chest with the leash connected in front. This worked like a charm because the dog couldn't pull me. BUT ... the hard part was getting it back on Diesel after his first outing with it. The next time I headed toward him with the harness, I found myself chasing him around the yard. He'd wait until I got almost close enough to reach him, then bolt away.

I moved on to Daisy. To put her harness on, each front leg had to be put through a separate section divided by a strip of fabric. This was a two-person job. How do you get a dog to lift one leg at a time?

I eventually learned to hold part of the harness under my neck while I put Daisy's second leg in. And, eventually, Diesel came to understand that the harness was a good thing. He would get his walk if he cooperated.

The tugging situation was fixed, but there were still two more issues that had to be resolved.

* * *

Howard had always been home to let these two in and out of the house when they needed a bathroom break. How could I possibly leave them inside all day when I went back to work?

I decided to have a doggie door installed in the back door, which would give them access to the fenced-in back yard. I figured they could let themselves in and out.

My brother Jimmy helped install it, and we introduced both dogs to the concept when he was done. Daisy, God bless her soul, got it right away. She poked her head through it to see what was on the other side, my brother called her to him and, boom, in one hop she was out.

Diesel, however, was highly suspicious of the thing. I dragged him across the kitchen to see it up close and personal, then shoved his head through the hole. On the other side, he saw Jimmy and Daisy looking at him, but he refused to look at them. As is often the case with Diesel, he wasn't having it. It was too different, too risky. This dog does *not* like change.

I had his head out the doggie door, but I could not figure out how to get him to put a leg through it. He was going to have to decide to do this on his own. We left him alone to figure it out.

Later that evening, as Daisy was busying herself going in and out, in and out, Diesel stuck his head out the doggie door to watch Daisy play. He stood there for a while, then turned in for the night. The next morning he poked his head out again.

Finally, he gingerly took a step over the doggie door threshold and got one foot out. He stood there for long moments while he considered his next move. It was either put another leg out or pull the first leg back in.

In the end, he agreed to go for it. Over time, he grew willing to leave the house by means of the dog door. But come back in? Not on your life. He stands on the porch and barks until someone gets up and lets him in.

\* \* \*

My other issue with these two was the fact they actually preferred to be out front. Diesel is nosy and wants to keep track of everything going on in the neighborhood, and Daisy goes where Diesel goes.

There's no fence out front, of course. At first, I tried tying them out, but they tangled themselves on the porch banisters, the bushes and each other. This wasn't going to work.

Thus it was that I ventured into the world of the electric fence.

Money again. For $1,200 I could keep these two in the front yard and wouldn't have to untangle them. After a couple of shocks, both dogs learned quickly where their boundaries were.

The fence, though, created bridge trolls out of my two dogs. I half expected them to stop everyone on the street and ask for the password.

Everyone who sets foot onto Oxford Road gets greeted by the barking Diesel and Daisy, who match them step for step while they walk past our house. It can be intimidating, I'm sure, but all Diesel wants is for someone to stop and scratch his butt.

And of course my front lawn looks like the worst sort of trash lives here. My flowers and shrubs are dug up and chewed, there are a dozen or so holes in the yard along with torn up stuffed animals (stolen from Trisha's room), discarded bones, and chewed up lawn ornaments and furniture cushions.

Neighbors say my lawn is where stuffed animals go to die.

\* \* \*

The winter after Howard died, I began to find my clothes outside on the back lawn – shoes, stockings, underpants, bra, socks. After the spring thaw that first year, I found clothes that had been buried in snow over the winter.

It was Diesel.

His criminal activity expanded to outright theft when visitors were in the house. It started when my cousin's son Charlie came to visit. When he arrived, he had a bag full of his personal items including a cell phone, which he put down on the bench just inside our front door.

Eventually, I noticed Diesel going out the dog door, coming back in (on his own for a change), going out, coming in. I went outside to investigate. And there, among other stolen items in the snow, I saw a mangled cell phone. Diesel had rummaged through Charlie's bag and helped himself to the kid's belongings.

Diesel's stealing escalated after that. They say that during grief those deeply affected find great comfort in shopping – buying things for themselves, for their house, their kids. It lightens the mood, at least for a little while. I'd like to give Diesel the benefit of the doubt and think that perhaps he was "shopping," but in my heart I knew he was just a thief.

I have found him by the front door countless times, head tucked to one said (a clear give-away that he's hiding something) and, sure enough, there in his mouth is a visitor's wallet, hairbrush, glove, scarf, sandwich, phone, boot, book ... nothing is safe.

I have also had to lay out some big money because of his shoplifting. Do you know how much Ugg boots cost?!

Eventually, I posted a sign by the front door:

THIS IS A WARNING!
Do not leave your shoes, gloves, hats, phones
or other items within reach of Diesel.
If you do and he gets them, I will not replace them.
In addition, do not leave your knapsacks, backpacks or
pocketbooks unzipped or otherwise open –
he will take something!

In truth, though, I'd rather have Diesel shoplifting than lying at the top of the stairs with his head on his paws, sighing his heartbreak for Howard.

\* \* \*

## Jack and the Buttered Rolls

There's one more short story about the dogs that I'd like to add here, but it really says more about my family, particularly my father Jack, than about the dogs.

Like most people who live in Goshen – a village without a grocery store – I find myself going into Kwik Stop two or three times a day. So do my parents and my sister Kathy. Making cupcakes at the last minute? Run down to Kwik Stop. One of the dogs threw up and there are no paper towels in the house? Run down to Kwik Stop.

Needless to say, the staff down there knows everyone in town although they don't necessarily know who's related to whom.

One day toward the end of the summer after the shooting, Kathy and I happened show up there at the same time. We saw each other and kissed hello. She had her two daughters with her, and I kissed them hello, too. Yes, in my family, we kiss hello even if we just saw each other yesterday and, yes, even in Kwik Stop. Kisses are mandatory, especially since Howie died.

Someone working there – probably Theresa – said, "You two know each other?" and we both said, "Yes, we're sisters!" Other workers in the store soon got involved in the conversation and it was interesting to see their reaction, especially after the previous few months in our lives. We were local celebrities in a weird sort of way.

Then my dad walked in, and we did what we always do – kissed each other. Kathy and Dad kissed, he kissed the girls, and Dad and I kissed. Again, the staff at Kwik Stop knew who my dad was but didn't know we were related.

"Is that *your* dad?" Theresa wanted to know.

We all shouted, "Yes!"

"Oh my God, it's *your* dogs he buys the buttered rolls for every morning?!"

"Yes!"

Let me explain.

For years, my father had stopped into Kwik Stop every morning for his coffee. He was a regular, and the coffee purchase was regular, too.

Then shortly after Howard's death when Diesel was so depressed, my dad began a new ritual. Suddenly he was buying buttered rolls tin addition to his coffee.

At some point, he explained that the rolls were for his daughter's dogs. In a small town, a change in habit of such magnitude must be explained.

Five years later, my dad still makes this daily purchase for Diesel and Daisy. He arrives at Kwik Stop, gets his coffee and the buttered rolls, and then heads over to 10 Oxford Road.

Of course a few things have changed in five years. The dogs used stand by the door to await his arrival. There would be crying and whining and spinning and prancing when he pulled up in the driveway.

Now, though, they take my father for granted and consider the buttered rolls their due. They arise from my bed only after Dad gets in the door. Sometimes Diesel wants room service and doesn't even bother getting off the bed when my father arrives.

I had a serious talk with Diesel about how rude this is.

It did no good.

One last thing about my father Jack. There is always a buttered roll sitting on the kitchen counter when I get home from work.

That one is for me.

# 15

# Diesel's Story

## *As Told by Luke*

*The Man*

As the man moved slowly down Oxford Road, his tall wooden walking stick clicked on the pavement. He took his unlit cigar out of his mouth and spit onto the side of the road. The man looked down at Diesel, and the golden retriever looked up at him.

Diesel could see the sadness in the man's eyes. As they began walking again, he heard his owner begin to mumble to himself.

The dog had noticed lately that something was wrong with his owner. He was gone less often, and when he was home he was hidden away in his bedroom.

Lately, the man had started talking to himself whenever he was alone. Although Diesel was only a dog, he could see the man was thinking something scary.

Something was very wrong.

Despite the disheartening change that had taken place in Diesel's owner, the dog saw a silver lining as dogs always seem to do. The man was home a lot now, and this meant Diesel no longer had to spend the day by himself. Instead, he could spend time with his owner. That made Diesel happy even if it meant lying next to the bed all day.

At the end of Oxford Road, the man turned right. Whenever his owner took Diesel to the right, the dog knew it would be a short walk around the block instead of the usual journey into town. Diesel would rather have a long walk, but as long as he was with the man he was happy.

When they returned to their house, the man bent down to pet his dog. As the sun set on Oxford Road, Diesel and his owner could be seen sitting together on their front porch.

Diesel was happy, and his owner was mumbling.

*Shiny, Metal Puzzles*

The man was getting worse. His self-talk had become constant whenever he was alone, and he rarely left the house anymore. Diesel had become afraid to leave the man's side and was with him whenever the rest of the family was out.

The man's children did not seem to notice his recent odd behavior, but Diesel could see that his wife did. Over the past week, the man and his wife had been having hushed arguments in their bedroom. The woman did not want her children to know their dad's condition was worsening. She pleaded with him to tell her what was wrong. Diesel watched her ask this question many times, but the man never answered.

During the day, while his family was away, the man was bored. At least that's what Diesel thought. It was the only explanation the dog could come up with when the man began spending most of his days with his shiny, metal toys, taking them apart and putting them back together.

Over and over again, the man would take out his puzzles and disassemble them on his bed. Then he would scrub every part until they were all spotless, and then he'd reassemble them.

Diesel didn't find this very interesting, but he noticed that the man paid more attention to one of these objects than he did to all the others. He began keeping that particular one in his closet instead of returning it to the attic with the rest. Sometimes he would take it out of its box just to hold it and stare at it.

Diesel didn't like the way the man looked at his favorite metal puzzle. Diesel didn't like the way he sometimes pointed it at himself.

*The Gate*

The kids were home from school that day. Diesel noticed that happened occasionally. Although the man stayed in his bed, the rest of the family was quite active. The man's children walked into the bedroom once in a while to talk to their father.

The man's son brought him a sandwich. Peanut butter and jelly on toast. The man shared it with Diesel.

By two that afternoon, the chores were done and the house was quiet. The family said goodbye to Diesel and the man in bed, and then they left. But once the wife and children were gone, the man became active.

He spent some time writing on a small piece of notebook paper. Then he took out his favorite puzzle and laid it on the bed.

It wasn't until he grabbed Diesel by the collar that the dog realized something was very off. Diesel was led down to the living room at the bottom of the house, and a gate was wedged across the stairwell.

Diesel felt confused. The dog did not know why the man would lock him downstairs. Had he done something wrong? Diesel began to bark. He heard the man call down, "Everything will be okay, Diesel. It'll be okay ..."

The sound left Diesel reeling.

When he tried to bark he could not hear himself over the ringing in his ears. The dog wobbled over to one corner of the room and lay down, covering his ears with his paws. It took a while for the ringing to fade and, when it finally did, all was silent except for the man.

Diesel could hear him wheezing upstairs and, although he could not see the man, he knew he was hurt. He could hear the man's pain with every breath.

Diesel wanted desperately to climb the stairs and help the man, but the gate prevented him from reaching even the first step.

*Sirens*

Diesel was trapped behind the gate for what seemed like an eternity. When the man's family finally returned home, things only got worse. The man's son and daughter entered the house, but they didn't let Diesel out. And they didn't go upstairs to see their father.

Instead, they walked straight to the kitchen. Diesel could hear the messages on the phone begin to play. Their mother, however, was much more perceptive. The instant she spotted Diesel behind the gate, her eyes widened in panic.

She knew something was wrong, and so did Diesel.

Next, there was a scream. The woman was shouting, "Howie, what did you do?" Diesel heard her yelling for help. He could hear the children run up the stairs toward the bedroom, but she stopped them before they could enter. She gave them instructions in a stern and controlled voice.

Suddenly, the gate was removed and Diesel was led toward the back door. Then someone pulled him onto the back porch by his collar. Diesel turned around to head back into the house so he could reach the man, but the door was closed in his face.

His ears began to hurt again as sirens screamed their way toward Oxford Road.

Diesel stood at the side of the house and watched through the chain-link fence as big red trucks parked along the street. He saw two large, box-shaped vehicles park in the front of the house. There were so many people – dozens of people on the street and in the house – but Diesel could not see his family.

The children had been taken to a neighbor's back yard so they would not have to see the man being carried out on a stretcher with his head wrapped in white and a tube in his mouth.

But Diesel could see. He saw the man.

*Dressed in Black*

The following week was full of extremes.

Diesel's family was rarely home, but when they were, other people were with them. Everyone seemed numb. To Diesel, it seemed like no one had noticed the absence of the man.

On the fourth day, though, everyone finally broke down. Even the dog could see the family's hope had been shattered. That weekend the family left the house every morning, dressed in black and crying.

Diesel had not seen the man in more than a week, and he began to wonder when he would come back.

*The Truck*

Days melted into weeks and the man had still not returned.

His large, gray Ford truck remained in the driveway, exactly where the man had left it the last time he and Diesel had gone to town.

The man's wife became concerned about the truck. The man had always made sure to take care of it, but if it continued to sit idle and unused, the weather could begin to damage it.

The woman's brother came to do something with the truck. She led Diesel inside as the brother started the man's truck and drove it down Oxford Road. After the brother and the truck were gone, she let Diesel go back into the front yard.

Pretty soon, Diesel heard the sound, and he could not believe his ears.

It was the man's truck! He was finally coming home! As the truck turned the corner, Diesel could hear the familiar sound of it down shifting. He began barking wildly with excitement. His owner was finally returning!

The truck pulled into the driveway and stopped. Diesel eagerly sat outside the driver's door to greet his friend. But the person who stepped out was not the man. It was the woman's brother.

And then he knew. His owner was gone and was not coming back.

Diesel walked to the bushes that lined the house with his head down low. He sank heavily to the ground. The dog seemed to deflate as he crawled beneath the largest bush.

The man was gone, and Diesel was lonely.

*Diesel*

# 16

## People Say the Damndest Things

I guess I didn't really need Howard to shoot himself to figure out that people really do say some of the damndest things.

To be kind, I understand that it's hard to know just what the right thing *is* to say to a grieving widow of a suicide. Or to the grieving widow's family and friends. On the other hand, what's wrong with just being quiet when you don't know what to say?

To imagine that we weren't the topic of conversation would be foolish. Of course we were. I'm sure the kids and I came up at many family dinner tables. I didn't often dwell on the question of what others thought of us. It honestly didn't matter until about two years out when my friends and relatives felt that I was stronger and decided it was okay to tell me some of the very callous things others were saying.

Can you imagine saying to one of my sisters, "Well, we heard Trish was going to divorce him so he shot himself."

Or how about, "I cannot believe Howard would leave that legacy for his children"?

Or, "I heard he had a full arsenal in that house."

I got to the point where, when someone began reporting these comments to me, I'd say stop. Hearing it only made matters worse.

But I didn't need those close to me to tell me what others were saying. At some point – even early on – a few people decided it would be a good idea to give me unsolicited advice and to offer their commentary on Howard, the kids and me.

At about one and a half years out, someone told me it was time for me to start "thinking of others." Really?

Okay, so here I was, a forty-five-year-old widow just emerging from the shock of finding her husband with the right side of his head blown off, and two teenagers – *teenagers* – who still hadn't even begun to process what happened, and this person tells me I have to start thinking of others?

I was actually at a loss for words. Sometimes I wish I could go back and conjure just the right response to idiots like that.

I've also heard a remarkable mix of questions from people whose curiosity about the macabre nature of Howard's death apparently overcame any common sense and decency they might have had.

Consider the following:
*Was there blood all over the room?*
*How could you possibly touch him?*
*Who cleaned up the room?*
*How do you sleep in that room?*
*How could you possibly live in that house?*
*How could you make your kids live in that house?*
*Why did you have an open casket?*
*How come no one could see the bullet wound in his head at the wake?*
*How could you not be mad forever at him?* (That one's not such a bad question, actually.)
*Don't you just want to die?*

And there was no shortage of advice from people who had absolutely no experience with suicide but who thought they knew best none-the-less:
*You've got to move out of that house.*
*Don't even think about getting remarried.*
*Just worry about the kids – that's your job now and for the rest of your life.*
*Well, I know I* would *never go out on a date at all – ever. My kids would come first until I died.*

*Suicide is the most selfish act in the world; I pray he goes to hell.* (How nice and thoughtful.)

I also discovered that some people think they're amateur psychiatrists, and they often formed onclusions about my emotional state after a five-minute conversation down at the Kwik Stop.

To those people I would have liked to say (but didn't):
*Kwik Stop isn't exactly the right place for true confessions – there's not even a couch here.*
Or, *I'm lying to you when I say all is well. Don't be fooled if I come across as a solid, healthy, functioning Rock of Gibraltar. I'm going home now and having a meltdown.*

As much as I wanted to speak honestly, I was terrified that, if I started, I wouldn't stop. It was far too scary to contemplate letting loose my dark, deep and violent emotions standing in the middle of a deli.

So when people said to me, "How *are* you," and I said, "I'm okay," it was not at all helpful for them to say, "No, *really*, how *are* you?"

Maybe I handled that wrong. Maybe I should have said, "Actually, I feel that at any moment, I will turn to dust and simply fall away into a million tiny pieces with the next step I take."

Or, "I feel dead and hopeless … I feel like I'm suffocating … I'm hanging on by the slenderest of threads."

Maybe I thought I would be a disappointment if I spilled my guts on the floor standing right there in front of a deli counter full of macaroni, potato and egg salad.

More likely, I knew I would be disappointed in the platitudes that were sure to follow: "Oh, I'm so sorry, but time heals all wounds … Oh, I wish there were something I could do for you … Oh, you're strong – you'll be fine."

I didn't want to hear that shit. But, really, what was I expecting?

I suppose, in the delusional part of my mind, I was expecting these people with all of their advice and clichés to make it all better. In my real mind, though, I knew that wouldn't happen any more than I'd see Howard rise from the dead.

I saw a news item about a pilot who had a panic attack on his airplane. Perhaps that is exactly what I thought I would end up doing if I ever did answer truthfully when some asked, "How are you *really* doing?" Perhaps I would start screaming like that pilot did and begin spewing crazy talk like, "We have Iran ... we have Israel." I think I was afraid that if I ever went that far into the grief I would never come out whole.

I imagine people have gone crazy with grief and I truly didn't want to go there. I had too much to do. On the other hand, crazy would have been a welcome relief.

* * *

It was more than four years after Howard's death that I began discussing some of the graphic details of his suicide with family and close friends – finding him, missing him, the things that seemed too raw to discuss for most of these past years, topics that if I ventured into I was afraid I might not find my way out again. I guess it began to feel safer. I finally felt that I wouldn't die from discussing it, that it was okay if *I* said the damndest things, too.

It was at my sister Ann's during her daughter Jessica's twenty-first birthday party that I finally spoke to my sisters, for the very first time, about finding Howard. I described what he looked like, the condition of the room, what I did, what I said. It was almost like an out of body experience, this telling.

Even as I was telling them about this – my sisters who love me and know me – I was wondering, do they think I'm crazy? Do they wonder how I could just say these words? Do they wonder if they shouldn't stand too close to me right now? Do they wonder if they should say anything?

I really don't know what they thought. I don't remember if they spoke or just listened. It was hard enough just getting my words out.

That's all I remember about that.

# 17

## Grief Journal
*The Second Year*

*June 01, 2008*

Hi Howard.

Well, as you know, all the one-year anniversaries have come and gone: a year from when you shot yourself; a year from when you died; and now, today, it will be a year ago that all of the organ recipients got their new organs.

Because of you, Howard. Yeah!

*June 08, 2008*

Hi Howard.

I was wondering yesterday as I walked the dogs (it was almost dark) what you were doing right then up in heaven. Who were you walking with and talking to?

I think of you most often as evening rolls around. Something about the evening sky, with light and dark fighting it out, brings you to my mind. The smells, the birds, people out for a walk – they create such a longing in my heart for you.

Sara next door wrote a card with a memory of you in it. She recalled how she would look out and see you sitting on the front steps with me. Funny how certain memories burn themselves deep within you and can stir such emotions inside.

Got to go. Life would be so much easier if you were here, Howard. I get so overwhelmed thinking of all I have to do – the kids, the house, the yard, the bills, the cleaning, the pool, the cars, the insurance, school, working – and all the things the kids need to learn like sex education (!) and driving.

I have no idea how I am going to be successful at any of this. I just don't know.

June 09, 2008

I am tired!

I am tired of trying to live each day as if it was okay. As if we were okay. As if there is hope and life to look forward to.

It's not okay. It's a chore every single minute I am awake to keep it going. Do the lawn, laundry, dishes, clothes, vacuuming, mopping; walk the dogs, feed the dogs, shop, drive the kids, put away, take out, clean the counters. The list goes on, and what for? What in the world for? So I can face another day doing the same mindless things, pretending it's okay?

It's not okay, God, and if it's ever going to be okay, you will have to make it okay. You say whomever calls upon you will receive an answer. I'm calling, God. I'm calling and screaming and crying.

Where are you? Are you in control? Do you have a plan? Could you at least let me in on the plan a little? Can you give me some hope? Anything to let me know it will be okay, the kids will be okay, and I can rest and trust you?

*The sign I asked for more than one year ago and continue to ask for – please, please make it something of wonder, of amazement so that I CAN FINALLY GET SOME REST! PLEASE PLEASE PLEASE.*

June 15, 2008<br>Father's Day

*Our second Father's Day without you, Howard. It's still so very sad! But for you in heaven, Howard, this is most likely the second-best Father's Day you have ever had.*

*And our babies (perhaps there were two of them?) get to have you right next to them. I'm happy for them but sad for Trisha and Luke, my babies here – stuck here in a sin-filled, gross, evil and heart-breaking world.*

June 16, 2008

Hi Howard.

Had a long talk with Diane tonight as always about you, our situation here since you died, my life and getting on with things. We talked about my always feeling the need to check in with family and friends about what I do and when I do it. This came up because I've been considering going to visit John S. in Colorado. He responded to an e-mail I sent him and, boy, did he ever give it to me! I feel like an idiot and hope I didn't ruin my chances. But even if I did, I feel it was something God wanted me to learn. Even if John and I don't work out, it was a much needed (and difficult) lesson.

I have to get on with things. I have to pray and then trust my instincts that it is God and the Holy Spirit talking to me.

## Things I Know God Has Done

I prayed ten years ago, Howard, about leaving you. Your depression was great and your drinking was BIG and interfering in our lives.

Diane instructed me back then to pray to God for a change in my heart and the courage to stay with you and be faithful to you and our marriage.

Do you know, God did just that? I remember having such a change in heart toward you – it didn't happen overnight, but I fell in love with you again. I had a kinder feeling toward you and that is why we remained married another ten years. But, you know, the year before you died was so, so difficult and I grew weary.

I guess God's answer was not to change anything down here but to allow you to return to him up there.

June 16, 2008

*Piglet sidled up to Pooh from behind.*
*"Pooh," he whispered.*
*"Yes Piglet?"*
*"Nothing," said Piglet, taking Pooh's paw. "I just wanted to be sure of you."*

*"God?" I whispered.*
*"Yes, Patricia."*
*"Nothing, God," I said, trying to touch Him. "I just wanted to be sure of you."*

*With no hand to hold and no skin to feel*
*How do we know you are near?*
*With no eyes to look into and no arms to feel your hug*
*How do we know you care?*

*With no spoken word to hear and no breath to feel*
*How do we know, God, we belong to you?*
*How do we know?*

July 11, 2008

*I walk again through Goshen village*
*Two dogs in tow*
*One pulling one way*
*The other going her own way*
*Here I am caught in the middle*
*Having no idea which way to go myself*

*I try to maintain some kind of order*
*By keeping their leashes untangled and*

*Keeping my feet on the ground*
*Every so often Daisy cuts me off*
*I don't usually anticipate this as I*
*Cannot see her with her black fur in the night*
*All of a sudden she is underfoot*
*Tripping me*
*And then I trip Diesel*

July 23, 2008

## Almost Feel It

*Almost feel it*
*Almost touch it*
*It rests deep in my soul*
*My God is in control.*
*His movement*
*His voice*
*His reassurance in His plan.*
*Lay it all at the cross*
*Take His hand*
*Let Him lead you along*
*Whatever road that He takes*
*"No matter what your eyes see,"*
*He says,*
*"Keep them on me."*
*So He leads and we stumble*
*Often veering away*
*His hand gently pulls and pushes*
*To help us on the right way.*
*He laughs at our blunders*
*He chides our deliberate forays*
*Nonetheless, He loves us still*
*For the duration of our days.*

*Oh God, may my calls to you*
*Be answered each day*
*May my disappointment in life*
*Be brushed away.*
*By your love and your plan*
*For each are there*
*Help me take your hand, Lord*
*And live my life knowing you care.*

*October 17, 2008*

Trisha came to me with a picture she drew. "Silent Hope," she called it.

It's a teddy bear with its mouth covered by a scarf. There is a tear in one eye and a heart in the other eye. In one corner there's a dead flower, and in the other corner a flower blooming.

To see such opposite emotions in this picture drawn by my daughter makes me lose my breath – literally. How does a mom fix this? How can a mom take this on? How can a mom love this away? I cannot. I wait on God. I wait and wait.

I've searched countless nights for a falling star. I don't remember when I started asking God for this; it was soon after Howard died. I ask every time I look up at the night sky.

"God, if everything is going to be okay, please let me see a falling star ... God, if Howard is walking right alongside Jesus, please let me see a falling star ... God, if I'm not going to be alone, please let me see a falling star ... God, if Trisha and Luke are going to be okay, please let me see a falling star."

When will He answer me? Just a quick, short answer is all I ask. Just the streak of a falling star. I'm not asking for more than that, Lord. When will you answer?

*November 11, 2008*

*Well, Howard, today is Luke's birthday. I wonder if you know that up in heaven?*

*He is sixteen years old. What an awesome kid we have here, but it's so difficult thinking of Luke at sixteen with no dad here with him. No father to go to practices with, to toss a ball with, to talk to. I wonder if you thought of that at all when you killed yourself.*

*I pray God will just send one man – just one guy who gets it and gives a hoot. Someone for me to love, but also someone who empathizes with the kids and could make a difference by being a father figure. Having a strong, solid, moral man in our lives would benefit all three of us tremendously. I sense Luke would respond so positively to someone taking an interest in him and his family. Trisha would respond slowly but with a sense of relief, I think.*

*Do I have enough to offer a man so that he would feel it was worthwhile extending himself to us? I don't think so. In this world, looks matter the most followed by money, neither of which I have very much of.*

*Still, God, please, please bring this dream to fruition. I don't want to be sitting here five years from now alone. The kids would not do well with that, and neither would I.*

*Howard, our birthdays, holidays and celebrations will forever be damaged by your killing yourself. There is no getting around that. You have left us with immeasurable pain. That's what you left behind for us.*

*It's Luke's sixteenth birthday, Howard. Where are you?*

*November 25, 2008*

*You think the worse thing he could have done was to die.*
*Then you realize he's not coming back.*

*November 25, 2008*

It's November again.

I remember this time last year. It's when I finally lost it. I finally crumbled into a heap of pain and weeping. I remember exactly when it started, on my way home from the first Worker's Compensation hearing I had to go to after Howard died.

I cried for weeks after that. It lasted all through the holidays into my knee surgery. I can remember that, and I know that I am somewhat better now. There are a few differences.

One is that I am healthier. Of course, some ulcer medication and the gallbladder removal have a lot to do with that, but so does my commitment to working out and staying in shape. I can't let myself go. If I had to live with myself as an overweight, out-of-shape, forty-six-year-old widow, I would never make it. If I let "me" go, then Howard's suicide wins.

Unfortunately, the confidence this gives me is shaky. I dated someone – just four times. I really liked him, actually, but he stopped calling. Obviously, this means I should be better looking, skinnier, funnier, smarter, richer, younger. Thus, I lose.

Another way I am different from a year ago is I cry less. Mostly, I cry about three times a month now. Not every day anymore.

I now have periods when I don't think about Howard. I can actually watch a movie with the kids and not think of Howard the whole time. I can walk the dogs with my iPod on and think of meeting someone and having fun. I can think of the kids and their struggles and not blame it all on Howard.

But still, I go back to it. I go back to thinking about Howard's suicide. When I do this going back, sometimes I can grit my teeth and say, No, no, I am not giving in. Other times, I just want to take a Tylenol PM and go to bed. Other times I cry. Sometimes I could throw a dish straight through the front window, but I don't. It would be too much trouble to get it fixed.

*I notice I am not so angry anymore. A year ago, I was often angry because Howard left me with so much crap to do – the shed, the basement, the pool, the lawn, the house, the pellet stove, the furnace, the damn truck, the dogs, the kids, the bills. He left me with such a huge mess.*

*So now, here I am, angry again. Damn.*

*November 25, 2008*

*I have a desire, so deep and so strong, to fall in love again. I don't know if it's because of my pain from losing Howard, or is it just a real, true desire?*

*The risks of getting out there and looking for someone are so, so large. You risk rejection. You risk making a mistake. You risk falling back into depression if things don't work out. You risk getting your heart broken. You risk losing hope.*

*We watched a movie last night called "The Ghost and the Darkness." One line Mr. Remington says is, "You just got hit. Now, whether or not you get up is up to you."*

*I want to get up. I want the kids to get up. I want God to tell me it's okay to get up. I want to know God is there to help us get up. I want another life partner to get up for and stay up with me!*

# 18

# Carnival Dating

Carnival dating. That's what one of my friends called it when I described my suitors, presumably because some of the men who answered my match.com ad might well have had gainful employment in a side show.

What an eye-opener it was to be dating again at the age of forty-seven after twenty years of marriage. I had been in love with only one man. I was Luke and Trisha's mom, Howard's widow, and then me. How did I even know who I was? How did I know what kind of man I'd like to meet?

Almost from the earliest days after Howard died, I knew I didn't want to be alone for the rest of my life, but that is a very different thing from wanting to go out on a date – or even knowing how to go about doing such a thing.

In fact, the idea of dating didn't really occur to me until about eighteen months after Howard was buried in the ground. Then suddenly it was like a light switch got turned on. Everything, including my hormones and body parts, began to wake up. I wanted to hold hands, get hugged and hear I was someone special.

What the hell was I going to do with all of this now. I essentially had no dating experience. With Howard, I had simply fallen in love. How could I possibly attract another man? Was I pretty enough? Was I engaging, captivating, smart, funny, stable and sexy enough? I began to have very real fears about ending up alone.

I feltl just like I had when I was seventeen years old with no steady boyfriend when everyone else seemed to have one. I was back to feeling inadequate, fat, ugly, misshapen, stupid and awkward. Just great. Now, besides being an insecure widow, I was also an insecure teenager again.

I was assured and reassured by friends and family that there was *someone out there* for me. All I had to do was be patient.

Be patient? Were they serious? Two of my most challenging character traits are a) impatience and b) a sense of inadequacy. Things didn't exactly bode well for me under the circumstances.

I looked around for possible avenues to meeting men.

Singles events at my church were zero.

No community sock hops for singles, either.

The kids' parents were all married.

The neighbors were great friends but ... married.

Sitting on my front porch and waiting for Prince Charming to come strolling down the street wasn't working.

It looked like Diesel would be my one and only boyfriend.

Then someone suggested I hire a life coach – yes, there is such a thing and I actually found a life coach for widows, someone who could teach me how to date, how to be safe out there and how to have fun.

Fun! What on earth was that?

And so I eventually found myself signing up to meet men online, first on a Christian dating site, then on match.com.

\* \* \*

What an ordeal it was, that initial signing up. First, I discovered I had to come up with a user name, something that everyone would see and form a first impression about me. I struggled mightily for hours trying to come up with something top notch, something truly awesome, something guaranteed to attract notice.

Since my first effort at all this was on a Christian dating site, I figured what better way to truly nail it than to include a Bible verse in my user name. Brilliant! I thought surely I was the first single person on a Christian web site to ever think of this.

So I picked the verse that had become very meaningful after Howie died – "Be Not Afraid." It was great! It looked like this:

"benotafraid1"

And no one else had it! I was psyched.

Of course, it didn't take me long to figure out that no one – NO ONE – cares about user names. I would soon come to understand that it's all about your picture, stupid! And I would learn early on that if you don't have a picture posted, the only people contacting you are those who also don't have a picture. And guys without pictures are generally ... well, hiding something.

But during that initial effort at reaching out, I wasn't prepared to post a picture of myself right away, so I moved on. The next thing was to describe myself in two hundred words or less. I was to summarize myself – my personality, likes, dislikes, hobbies, interests, musical and literary taste, and what I was looking for in a partner.

This made me feel really rushed and impatient. How was I going to meet someone if I had to do all this work before I could even put my really cool user name out there?

I decided to see what some of the other women on the site had written about themselves. Bad move. They all had pictures. And they all were gorgeous! How could these beautiful women all be single? Where did they come from? Did they have to be on the same site as me? Why couldn't they leave these sites for us normal looking people? Couldn't they just go out to a restaurant or ShopRite and meet guys? Surely someone in the vegetable aisle would ask any one of them out on a date.

Well, back to me. I certainly wasn't going to meet anyone unless I finished my profile, so I moved on.

Okay, likes. Let's see. I like dogs, warm days, awesome music on my IPod while I am out walking four miles, swimming in the ocean, going to the movies, Bethel Woods, my family, laughing (duh), a great glass of white wine, working out and bird watching. When Luke read that, he said, "Oh yeah, the bird watching thing is going to get them!" I should have known better than to ask his opinion.

At least I didn't put in that I liked sunsets, travel and sitting by a cozy fire. Everyone with a pulse, it seems, likes those things.

Dislikes – snow, cold, running late, household items that break down (I felt like I was playing Jeopardy) gaining weight (scratch that one), liver (duh again), being alone (sounds too desperate) and running out of gas (who does?).

Next thing – work. That one was easy. By this point, I had returned to nursing in a dialysis unit, in Orange County. After a year as a nurse teacher, I went back to doing what I enjoyed and was good at.

Hobbies. Not too difficult, I thought at first. Until I realized I had none. Working out with kettlebells, reading and walking the dogs are *not* exactly hobbies. What single mom with two kids and a full-time job has a damn hobby?

I decided to peak again at the other women's profiles for this one. Imagine trying to cheat on my self-portrait. This was crazy. Still, I chose women who were similar to me in age and circumstance, and here is what I found out. Other women scuba dive, paint, sculpt, play piano, wear designer clothes (that's a hobby?) snowboard and surf.

Really? Good grief. I couldn't compete. Maybe I needed to develop a few hobbies before going on a dating website, but that could take a year or two. I didn't have that kind of time. Plus, what if I picked the wrong hobby? Like bee keeping. That sounds really cool to me, but would I want to date a guy who keeps bees? He'd probably wear that huge white suit and a Star Wars helmet and travel to bee shows. I would have to wear a white suit as well.

Okay, so here's what I finally ended up with:

*I am a 47-year-old widow with two awesome kids. I work as a full-time nurse administrator and have had a career as an RN for more than 22 years. I am an energetic, independent, self supporting, positive, funny, physical and emotionally healthy female who desires to meet the next great love of my life. I am a Christian and I do attend weekly services at my local Baptist church. I love to read, listen to music, go to the gym, garden, visit local venues and attend any live music and/or theatre event. I come from a large Irish Catholic family where you will find a ton of laughter, love and support. I love being physically active, and keeping in shape is very important to me. I desire to meet a man who is kind, generous, emotionally and spiritually healthy, looking for a long-term relationship and willing to devote the time needed to have one. I have no addictions, don't smoke and desire the same in a man.*

I thought that was pretty good. Straight to the point and easy to read. I soon found out what I was in for.

\* \* \*

My very first response was from a man who was, without any stretching of the truth, deformed. He really was. He'd obviously had major surgery on his upper and lower jaw plus his left eye was much smaller than the right.

I was dumbfounded. I didn't know what to make of this! I printed the picture and turned it every which way to see if perhaps there were shadows that could account for the appearance of deformities but, alas, no.

His user name was mycuprunnethover. God forgive me, I bet his cup runneth over whenever he tried to drink. I never said it out loud, but I thought it. I'm sorry.

He was fifty-two, never married, and wanted to meet "a woman who was physically beautiful with a beautiful personality as well. Someone who takes care of herself and is slim, a strong Christian woman who fully believes that God made man to be head of the household and his wife to love him."

And he sent me a smiley face.

Good grief.

One thing I did learn from this guy, though, was that if he could put his picture out there, maybe I should get over myself. At least I'm not deformed. True, I have a slightly large Irish nose, but it couldn't hold a candle to his physical issues.

I had Trisha take a picture of me sitting at my computer in the small hallway outside my bedroom. My hair looked good, and my smile was bright and cheery. Honestly, I thought it was very natural and happy looking. I had it posted on the website.

For those of you contemplating having a picture of yourself taken with your daughter's cell phone, please take note: Check the background.

The first message I received after posting my picture was, "I guess you love to clean – you have your vacuum in the picture with you."

I looked closely at the picture and, sure enough, there was the Electrolux canister vacuum standing proudly in the background. How did I miss that one? Well, I figured, at least it shows I clean.

The second response: "I like the paint roller and pan in the background –did you stop in the middle of painting to pose for a picture?"

Didn't notice that, either.

And a third response: "Is that dog dead in the background?"

Oh for crying out loud. I looked back at the picture and, sure enough, there was Daisy Mae stretched out on the floor in front of the vacuum like she'd just passed out – or passed on.

This was so embarrassing but, come on, didn't they even look at *me*? Those guys had to have studied the picture. Didn't they notice my nice smile?

On the other hand, the more I looked at the picture, the bigger my nose got.

\* \* \*

Clearly, though, based on the kinds of responses I got during the long months I ran a personal ad on that Christian site, then on Match.com, there had to be a water mark on my profile I did not see.

At various times, my profile must have included the following words:

*If you have had back surgery, certainly call me – been there, done that, and oh how I want to do that again! You only take four Percocet per day, so you are really doing well with that!*

*If you are currently on disability, please call. I would like nothing more than to date someone who doesn't work and has no intentions of working again. Like you say, this leaves you tons of time to see me.*

*Also, if you are laid off – but hope to get a job soon! – call me. I have a job, a really good one, and of course I don't mind supporting you because you are such a great catch.*

*If you drive a Ford – preferably a 20-year-old Crown Vic that smells like an old man and is in need of a muffler, definitely give me a call.*

*If you cannot get over your ex-girlfriend – you know, the one you had to serve papers on to get her out of your house – definitely call me, woo me and snow me. Then after about eight weeks, feel free to dump me over the phone and move that bipolar, alcoholic beauty of yours back into the house. Heaven knows she is the better catch.*

*If your wife committed suicide, contact me. You know I am a widow so I would understand, of course. (Weirdly, I was contacted by four men whose wives had killed themselves and none of them knew about Howard. I didn't get it.)*

*If you are a good looking, divorced county worker, who could "really use a massage, how about it?" make sure you show up at my house so I can give you a rub down.*

*If your picture is of a great-looking Italian guy, it's perfectly okay if it was taken at least ten years ago and you're now fifty pounds heavier and have no neck.*

*If you have a bad case of ADHD and also kind of wave like a girl, give me a shout. Especially if you're also an alcoholic who's lost his driver's license and rides a bike to work.*

*If you whine, also just fine.*

* * *

Not all the men I met online were this awful. Some were actually very nice and a couple seemed like "possibles." But, for one reason or another, we just weren't meant for each other. We generally parted on friendly terms.

Still, I seemed to attract the wounded and needy. After a while, I learned to laugh on the inside with not a hint of it on the outside, but it caused a very painful sensation in my bladder and stomach.

I finally concluded that my heart wasn't in it, and this just wasn't going to be how I'd meet my new soul mate – or even a new, long-term friend. I made the decision to end my experiment with online dating as soon as my contract had run its course.

But guess what happened on my last week as a paying customer on match.com?

# 19

## Grief Journal
*Onward*

*April 25, 2009*

    *I heard on the radio this morning these words from a song: "It won't be like this for long ..."*
    *And I wondered, could that be for me? Could that be a message to tell me I won't be alone for long and the kids and I will find love, comfort, security, provision and protection from God and from the man God will send into my life?*
    *Oh, to think it may be so!!!* ☺

*April 25, 2009*

### My Walk To Meet You
*As I turn the corner up around the street*
*The road rises sharply and at the top we meet*
*Off ahead way beyond I see the sun setting slow*
*I stand still and watch as I feel the wind blow*
*Is that you who sends the hawk over my way?*

*Is that you in the smell of the lilacs today?*
*If ever we are to meet it would be on this hill*
*As the road rises up and the trees stand still*
*Diesel and Daisy stand beside me as if they know*
*If we all wait long enough with the wind you will show*
*Diesel sets his brown eyes straight ahead up the road*
*He must sense you by, sense the smell of your clothes*

*Walking to meet you*
*Where must I go*
*Wondering where you might be*
*Hoping it is there I can go*
*Just to see your handsome face*
*Touch the back of your hand*
*Fold myself into your shape*
*It was always a perfect place*

*November 10, 2009*

One day before Luke's seventeenth birthday, Howard. Can you believe it?

You've been gone thirty months – two and a half years. Each month I think, "No way it could get any worse" and, bam, it does. But I feel something different this week – maybe the tide is turning? Maybe, just maybe, the three of us can relax and take a breath. That's all I would love for Christmas – the chance to exhale and not tighten up thinking that just around the corner is another situation I have to deal with. Ahhhh, that would be so nice – twelve months of quiet.

Just to recap for you, Howard, since you left:

The first six months of walking around as if dead but still breathing

*November 2007 The compensation hearings start and I lose it around then*

*February 2008 Total knee replacement*

*Summer 2008 Both kids start to exhibit signs of depression*

*September 2008 I start a new full-time job and get really tired all the time*

*October 2008 Trisha starts acting out with cutting and it breaks my heart to see her so sad*

*November 2008 My gallbladder comes out*

*December 2008 The holidays are worse than the first ones*

*January 2009 Trisha is doing terrible and by early February she says she tried to kill herself but stopped; she goes to an adolescent psych unit for ten days*

*February 2009 Trisha comes home and works so hard on her school work; things might be getting better*

*May 2009 We learn that Trisha has severe hyperthyroidism and start weekly trips to a doc in Westchester*

*June 2009 I have terrible pain in my left ovary and have laparoscopic surgery to remove ovary and Fallopian tube*

*July 2009 I start yet another new job; I feel so lost, out of place and incompetent; am running out of steam*

*July 2009 Trisha has a nose job – it looks awesome; some good stuff for her*

*August 2009 Finally learn the cause of Trisha's hyperthyroidism is her acne medication*

*September 2009 I cannot keep watching Trisha and her stupid fifteen-year-old boyfriend*

*October 2009 Another surgery for me, this time an abdominal hernia repair*

*October 2009 Trisha has a devastating problem that brings heartache and despair all over again*

*On the other hand, there have been some positives:*

*Luke and Trisha have not failed any courses; they keep mostly A's and B's*

*As far as I know, both are not frequent users of alcohol or drugs; they just eat all the food*

*They still have a sense of humor*

*They seem to be starting to formulate goals and dreams and maybe even look forward to them*

*They have friends they enjoy*

*They still like to spend my money*

*Physically, Luke is fantastic*

*Physically, Trisha is still the same – catching everything that's in the wind but getting over it*

*They smile*

*They love Diesel and Daisy*

*They still go to counseling, even after two and a half years*

*New rooms*

*A car for Luke*

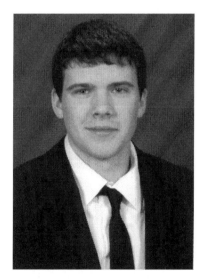

*Luke in his senior year of high school*

*February 26, 2012*

*Can you believe it's 2012 already?*

*And no, I have not found the man I still hope and pray God has set aside for me. And it hasn't been due to not wanting him and not searching for him – I have done both extensively over the past two years, and yet I sit here on my bed alone tonight re-reading my journal entries from 2007–2009 and wondering: Why am I still writing about being alone and lonely?*

*But you know what? I have come from the ground up to this level and the view is pretty good right now.*

*Trisha at her high school graduation*

*March 2012*

*Most of us have experienced the death of a close relative or friend. It is a natural part of life, so we are told; however, "natural" seems a funny word to describe something that is so life changing.*

As a registered nurse now for almost twenty-three years, I've seen death time and again. I've worked in the field of dialysis for most of those years, and each year I expect to see anywhere from twenty to forty of our patients die. So I have actually known hundreds of patients who have died.

So, yes, death is a natural occurrence in my life. But nothing seems natural about Howard's death. If anything, it seems totally alien and unnatural to the core. How could he possibly be here one minute and gone the next? It still causes a visceral gut reaction in me when I think of it that way.

Prior to Howard's death, I had several relatives who died. Some seemed natural, such as when my eighty-two-year-old old grandfather died. All of my grandparents were dead by 2007 as well as a dear uncle, aunt and cousin.

But other deaths, like my seventeen-year-old cousin and my two miscarriages – not natural at all. Unexpected and devastating.

All those deaths did impact my life to some extent. Some of my patients' deaths have also had an impact. No death in my life has been a ho-hum event. But some deaths, unlike others, dramatically change your life.

When Howard died, everything changed, even the color of the sky. And there was nothing natural about it at all.

February 2012

## More Than Anything

My *More Than Anythings* started the moment I found Howard on the floor. I remember screaming to him, "I don't understand Howard – what the hell happened? What did you do?" I wanted more than anything to figure out what the hell was going on. Then I moved on to wanting more than anything to get out of the bedroom as I heard Luke running up the stairs.

I wanted more than anything to get Craig to hear me screaming so he would come over. More than anything, I desperately needed the 911 operator to stop asking me who was in the house and just for crying out loud get the ambulance over to us.

I continued to want a lot of things more than anything that day. More than anything I wanted my parents and my siblings; I wanted someone to go in and be with Howard; I wanted my brother Jimmy to answer the phone; I wanted the kids to be taken away and kept safe; I wanted to shake Howard until he woke up.

More than anything I wanted Howard to be okay when I got to Westchester Medical Center and that, when we walked into the ER, I would be told he'd been sent up for surgery. But when we learned he was still in the ER, I wanted more than anything to throw up, to run, to scream, to beat the shit out of him. When the ER doctor told me his injury was incompatible with life, I wanted more than anything for Howard to not live as a vegetable. I wanted more than anything to not be watching as my mother collapsed and said to my father, "My God, Jack, what are we going to do?"

In the end that day, I wanted more than anything to simply disappear.

My More than Anythings continued for more than five years. There were simple More than Anythings, such as more than anything I just wanted to get some sleep. More than anything I wanted to get rid of the feeling of nausea and burning that settled in my gut for two years.

My More Than Anythings were for a long time desperate cries for relief – a return to life without anxiety, panic and fear; to life without a cement-like depression; to a life of peace, comfort and perhaps amnesia; to a nice dream of Howard and perhaps a message from him as well.

To save the reader from the agony of having to read the words More Than Anything another hundred times, I will simply list them here by year:

No one would be surprised to learn the first year's list was mostly about just wishing Howard were back, pure and simple. I wished it all away.

*By the second year the list included wishing that the numbness would return, the depression would lift, the fear would release its grip; that the kids would simply just heal, that I would be normal, that we would all laugh a pure, deep-down belly laugh, that the vacant stare in the kids' eyes would disappear; that I could give a shit about something other than my situation.*

*In the next three years, I wished that Trisha did not want to kill herself, that Luke would talk about his pain so he could move past it, for time to pass swiftly so we could be that much closer to feeling whole again.*

*The third year was the worst for many reasons and in many ways. I had moved from numbing pain through life-crippling depression and was now in a place I would call mud. I was just stuck. Others' expectations of me were much higher now, but I felt stuck. I wished for a clear head, a clear thought, a self-directed idea to take shape and the courage to run with it. I wished for Trisha and Luke to enjoy school and friends, to not have to work so hard, to fall in love, to be unafraid of being alone.*

*More than anything now, I am thankful for Trisha's spirit, kindness, courage and love; for Luke's determination, humor, love of laughter and continued desire to do life; for God's protection over us these past five years.*

*And more than anything, I never want my children nor I to experience that much pain again in this life.*

*Please God, may it be so.*

# 20

# Gerard

My friends who knew I was working on this book have often said to me, so, have you met the last chapter yet?

I'm happy to report that I have. It happened my last week as a paying customer on match.com. I had used this dating service to its full advantage, and I was putting an end to it with mixed feelings. On one hand, I would never have met as many men as I did; on the other hand, I could happily live the rest of my life without meeting most of them again.

The men I would consider of above average intelligence and of a clean, moral, decent character would agree with what I'm about to say – finding "normal" on these dating sites was a great deal more difficult than I ever imagined.

Who knew there was so much dysfunction out there? Yes, none of us are perfect – we are, after all, human. But the dysfunction I speak of goes well beyond the average: alcoholism and other addictions; dishonesty; extremes of all sorts; questionable motives; motives I wouldn't even want to mention; liars who mislead and misrepresent; and people who were just plain weird.

Then there were men who had no clue what they wanted from a relationship; men who were still devastated over the loss of a spouse; men who were dripping with bitterness over a cheating wife; men in denial over a crazy girlfriend; men who wanted a mom; men who were bed-hopping and running on hormones; men who were leaving a third marriage and – gee! – could it possibly be that they're part of the problem?

Still, there was hope inside me. I just knew in my heart there was someone else for me – someone who would simply blow me away. Someone generous, kind, physical, healthy and something of a wiseass. I just knew this guy was looking for an Irish girl who was kind of like him.

I began looking outside the thirty-mile range I had usually set. I extended it to fifty miles. I figured there had to be someone worth driving fifty miles for.

Up came pages of guys from New Jersey. Hackettstown had quite a lot of men, and I wondered why. Were there more men than women in Hackettstown? Vernon also seemed to have a lot of single men. Most seemed to live in a townhouse at the foot of the ski mountain. Did that many fifty-plus-year-old guys actually ski?

It was two nights before my membership was to expire. I was ready to move on, but I figured, why not start winking at all the good-looking guys before signing off? (A wink is match.com's way of politely letting someone know you're interested.)

And then ... there he was. A man named Gerard. What a fantastic smile! How could I possibly know a smile is genuine from a photograph, you ask? You can see it in someone's eyes. This guy's smile lit up his face, and his eyes lit up the screen.

And he had a goatee! I am a sucker for a really well groomed goatee. In one picture he was standing with a sport coat on; another was a close-up one. Damn, he was handsome! In another, he was with a dog. (Must love dogs! Another plus.)

His profile was an easy read, and it held a hint of sarcasm – just enough to make me smile a little. He mentioned dogs – it happened to be his passion and his business. Wow. (I don't think he mentioned just how many dogs he owned, but I would find out on our first date.) He seemed intelligent without being annoying. His taste in music was okay.

So, without really thinking this would go anywhere, I decided to wink away at Mr. Handsome from Morris Plains, New Jersey, and not worry about the outcome.

Well, apparently Mr. Handsome saw my picture and thought I was very pretty and had a great smile and eyes. (Thank goodness for permanent makeup!) But he was sold on contacting me for another reason.

Here I was, a girl from Goshen, New York – the very place his dad used to take his family on vacation during summers when they were young. His dad loved harness racing, and for those unfamiliar with Goshen, it is the harness racing capital of the world – or at least it was during Gerard's youth.

Now here was a girl from Goshen of all places winking at him on match.com – a girl who would end up saying to herself after the first date, "Now *that* was a date and *that* is a man I would love to spend some time with."

And I did. It turned out that Gerard owns a successful dog grooming, training and day care business in Morris Plains. And it turned out that he had five dogs of his own. And a house. And he wasn't a liar or an alcoholic or even slightly weird. He was divorced (once), had no children, and drove a van with a lot of dog cages in the back.

I knew he was a keeper the first time he and I took Diesel and Daisy for a walk together. I always carry a plastic poop bag with me, for obvious reasons. Well, let me tell you what happened when Diesel found his spot. Gerard took the plastic bag from me and picked up the poop himself! And then he carried the bag the rest of the way home!

I couldn't help myself. "You are the best!" I told him. And he asked me what kind of man he would be if he let me carry a bag of dog shit around town.

That was it for me. I'm not sure just what did it for him, but I would never wink at another man again.

\* \* \*

Or course, is there ever perfection? Or clear, smooth sailing? Not for this girl! I am imagining God felt that, by 2012, my life had settled down enough to feel He could once again send some challenge my way. It seems to be a pattern with our Heavenly

Father – "Let's see. Trish has been a bit too calm lately. Let me throw a little something her way just to keep her on her toes."

Often the "little something" involved the kids, but this time it was Gerard who was sent my way.

Yes I love him madly. Yes, we clicked right from the start and fell in love. And yes, Gerard is a handful. I know he would describe me the same way, but for much different reasons.

We are vastly different in many ways. My insecurities are a stark contrast to his confidence. It is hard for me to live with the fact that my greatest flaw – insecurity – is what gets under his skin the most.

I have fallen in love with someone who not only can out-talk me, but to whom I must often say, "Would you please just be quiet for a minute?" I admit my tone isn't as polite as it looks on paper.

He says I give him way too much credit for "deep thinking." Most often, he says, he hasn't given something any thought at all. He lovingly ( I use that loosely) accuses me of thinking *too* much or reading into something that isn't there.

There is a great deal we do not agree on: sports teams; how far Cancun really is from California; whether he's really listening to me if he's not looking at me when I talk.

He *must* deliver most of his statements as absolute facts and has difficulty understanding that he really isn't always right. I've had to learn to speak up when I'm pretty sure he's wrong and I'm right. He still needs to learn *not* to say "Whatever" when I prove him wrong. As it turns out, I'm usually right.

He sleeps only four to five hours per night and expects me to do the same. Does this drive me crazy? Absolutely. At some point, I may have to fake a migraine or an allergy to his pillows so I can sleep undisturbed in another room.

I have trouble "reading" him. Does this annoy the hell out of him? Absolutely. I already see that I need to let this go a bit.

He beats me always at backgammon and I hate it. He has the luckiest dice rolls I have ever seen. He could have four gammon pieces left on the board, all four on one space. What happens? He rolls doubles for that space! He must take me gambling.

I beat him at some stupid Frisbee throwing game when we were first dating, and he hates even the memory of his humiliation. Plus, he beat me by only one – ONE! – goal in a three-game air hockey series. Me, a woman. He can't stand it.

It irks him that I lack the discipline to train my dogs properly – but I love them and am working on it. I think my lack of talent in this area not only confuses him but disappoints him.

It irks me when he asks me the same question several times in a row. I answer him the first time and almost every time thereafter, but inevitably he will ask again. Most days it cracks me up – some days I would like to crack him over the head.

I've been asked, "Why do you want to get married again? Just live together – just date! It's less complicated that way."

\* \* \*

Well, it's a good question. There are many valid and sensible reasons not to marry again.

But the reasons to get married far outweigh the downside. First, we are of the same mind – we both want to be married. We find that commitment is something to aspire to and to cherish.

Is commitment one of the biggest challenges in life? Absolutely. But what in life worth so much doesn't require work? And perhaps a little self-improvement? Being in a committed relationship forces me take a good look at my flaws, work on them, laugh at them and maybe eventually cut myself some slack in regards to them. And that's a two-way street.

Second, I believe we have both chosen wisely. We are so very good together. Yes, we have differences, but once the storm passes, we move on together.

Third, we are such good friends. We are friends first, then lovers and partners. This relationships is built on the lasting foundation of friendship.

Fourth, he makes me laugh, I make him laugh, I make myself laugh when I am with him, and he cracks himself up at my expense. When he ages (and I, of course, stay youthful looking), we will still make each other laugh. What could be better?

Fifth, I find him outrageously attractive, sexy and so appealing. He tells me I do the same for him. We don't know all the reasons why – who ever can fully explain such attraction? – but it doesn't matter. It works. And for the record, we are picky.

Sixth, his life and mine mesh. His five dogs and my two dogs, one cat and – oh – two kids! seem to click and thrive when put together.

And last – yes, we love each other. We truly do. And sometimes it is that simple.

I have many flaws. So does Gerard. Anyone can be on best behavior while dating for a month, four months, even a year. But the hard work begins when you take the step to live together.

Marriage takes it so much further. When people get married, they are stuck with each other, they really are. And basically they have to find a way to work out any differences they discover along the way, come hell or high water. And that is the good thing about marriage.

* * *

I met Gerard a few months before the five-year anniversary of Howard's suicide. And you know what he said to me less than two months after our first date? He said, "I love you more than anything."

I couldn't believe it. He turned my More Than Anythings completely upside down. Suddenly, instead of wishing something away, it became a wish of happiness, a declaration of love and of hope. It's more than anything I ever hoped for.

Gerard and I were married April 6, 2013. It was a most wonderful party.

More than anything now, I want what lies ahead. And I am so thankful we have made it through what lay behind.

*The wedding party: Luke, Trish, Gerard and Trisha*

# 21

# Grown Up

So here we are, six years out from Howard's death.

Certainly, our happiest year has been this past one with Gerard in our lives. And I'd love to be able to say that we've arrived at the "and they all lived happily ever after" chapter.

But as with all of life, we would be foolish to think that our struggles and trials are over. This sixth year has brought with it some unexpected issues and complications for Luke and Trisha, just as each of the previous five years did.

I've spent the good part of the years since Howard died attempting to get both Luke and Trisha to the place where they not only intellectually *know* there is life after death and they can be joyful again, but to get them to *feel* that in their hearts and souls. I want them in a place where their smiles come naturally and the light in their eyes shines.

Sometimes they actually are in that place. Sometimes. For that I'm so grateful.

And certainly, there are reasons to feel both proud and hopeful.

Trisha is so kind. She possesses endless empathy for those less fortunate and less able. She is slow to anger, and she has a great sense of humor. She is a great lover of animals. She is a wonderful friend to those who accept her friendship – she is a fantastic listener and quite possibly owns the biggest heart of gold I have ever encountered.

Luke, too, is so very kind and slow to anger. His sense of humor is awesome – very quick and dry. He is fun and plays well with others. His cousins adore him. He's an avid reader. When he works (note the word "when") he is a very hard worker. He is protective of his mom and sister.

They are both so smart, so loving, so sensitive, so forgiving. And they both have grown in areas that many adults never achieve.

They have a completely different world view than those who have not suffered a trauma, especially not at such a young age.

Still, this has been a year of ups and downs for them both. Yes, it has brought great things, but even happiness can be anxiety-producing. Change – even change from chronic sadness – can make people like Luke and Trisha anxious and vulnerable to depression.

Life is hard, for crying out loud, even when it's happy.

I have learned that when children experience extreme loss, they will grieve over and over again as they hit each period of growth. Each stage comes with a different type of loss.

Trisha and Luke re-experienced grief when they became older teens, and now they are re-experiencing it as young adults. It will probably hit them again when they are full-grown adults and when they have children of their own, perhaps when they least expect it.

*  *  *

Luke, normally a solid student at Temple University in Philadelphia, had his worst semester ever this past spring. Without question, he suffered a major depression and found it was the most difficult time he'd yet experienced in dealing with his father's death.

Suddenly, at the age of twenty, he couldn't get himself out of bed for the first time in his life.

He kept his depression to himself. I wasn't there to see it, and I missed the signs. He didn't want to burden his five housemates with it, and he certainly didn't want to weigh down his girlfriend Jamie with it.

I don't think he even knew what *it* was. This happens to many of us, I think. We might find ourselves in a place that could be anything from mild to major depression, yet we rationalize it away. "I'm just in a funk," we tell ourselves. We ignore it by working harder, faster and longer.

Or perhaps by trying to chase it away with alcohol, drugs or affairs.

But *it* remains. *It* stays because, just like an infected wound or diseased organ, *it* is a condition that has to be dealt with. Unfortunately, someone that depressed doesn't usually have the strength to seek out treatment and aggressively do battle with this condition.

And so, when Luke returned from school with his dismal, failing grades, I took control again. He is in therapy and on medication.

It is helping.

Trisha, too, had a less than stellar semester at SUNY Orange in Middletown. She has been moody, stubborn and – yes – depressed. In her case, because she was right under my nose, I could see it happening.

She, too, is back in therapy and on medication.

Even now, after all these years, some days are harder than others. For the first three years, I had to carry both Trisha and Luke's deep sadness as well as my own. I didn't know how to put it down.

Along the way, though, I learned that what worked with both my kids was to help them uncomplicate *it*. We would sit down, identify their symptoms, analyze the course of events that led up to the most recent bout of depression, and talk about the ways it was handicapping them.

I learned how to help them get to the root of the problem without placing blame.

And now, at year six, I find myself doing this again. But what I know now with far greater confidence than I once did is that we will find the solutions that work best for them.

Mostly, what we each have to do when we feel *it* trying to get a grip on us, is get a jump on *it*. Exercise, laugh, read, work with a passion at something we love to do, listen to music, seek out friends and family.

And mostly, *be not afraid.* Be who you were designed to be and allow your soul to emerge and soar.

That is what I tell my kids. My young adult children. My most incredible, wonderful children.

*Be not afraid*, my Luke and my Trisha.

## 22

## Luke Speaks
*Heroes In Tragedy*

My father's death was traumatic.

What happened on that horrid day left permanent scars on all who were there to witness it. But amidst the chaos and fear, there were people whose actions were no less than heroic for our struggling family. I am writing about them here so others can know how inspirational the actions of these heroes were to this teenaged boy.

\* \* \*

Craig Benson might well be taken for an average man. A regular guy. For years, he was our neighbor and a close family friend. On the day of my father's tragedy, however, he proved to be far more than an average person.

The image is still fresh in my mind. I can picture it as though I saw it only yesterday. It is an image of Craig Benson hurtling the fence that separated our back yards. When he heard my mother's piercing scream break the silence of our peaceful neighborhood, Craig – who was in the midst of entertaining company at his barbeque – turned without a second's hesitation and sprinted across his backyard. He had not the slightest idea of what he was running toward, but he ran, and then he launched himself over the chain link fence without breaking stride.

When he reached our house, he saw my father on the floor, bleeding out – a sight that would surely terrify most men into a panic. Craig, however, kept his cool and managed to practically carry my mother out of the house and away from the horrifying scene in her bedroom.

Craig was joined by a few more of our neighbors, whose actions that day were no less heroic. And after the house was empty and our family was gone, Scott Brinkley, our other neighbor, cleaned up the pools and spatters of blood that my father had left in my parent's bedroom.

He selflessly and courageously walked back into that room of horrors to scrub away the blood of one of his closest friends. I did not so much as glimpse the bedroom that day, but I can only imagine the horror that was within.

To this day I am inspired by and very grateful for my neighbors. I cannot even guess at the wounds they were left with. All I can say for sure is that Scott, Craig and the other neighbors of Oxford Road are true heroes.

\* \* \*

While some of the heroes to come out of that tragedy had been in front of us our whole lives, others came out of nowhere, or so it seemed.

Another act of heroism I will never forget came days after my father's passing. A friend I have not seen in many years became a hero in my eyes at my father's wake. Bobby came to the funeral home with the rest of my Little League baseball team.

The entire team very generously gave as much support as they could. However, unlike the rest of the team, Bobby stayed. He stayed to keep me company and cheer me up, which I have to say he did amazingly well. He was there for the entire wake, sitting by my side and making me smile. I think I would have fallen apart that day if he hadn't been there with me.

Although his presence may have seemed simple to him, it meant the world to me. I know, as few others do, that Bobby is a hero.

\* \* \*

Yet another act of heroism occurred during the week after my father shot himself. It was my baseball coach, Mr. Guarneiri –

one of the best coaches I've ever had – who was the hero this time.

That day I missed a huge game for our undefeated team. We played Monroe-Woodbury, a team that most people thought would crush us. But they didn't. Goshen pulled off the upset, beating Monroe 2-1.

I was devastated that I had not been there to help my team in such a crucial game, and this was just one more thing added to my trauma. Mr. G., however, completely turned my day around by doing something that could very well have gotten him fired.

On the bus ride back from Monroe, where the game had been played, my coach convinced the bus driver to make a detour to our house. Most schools strictly forbid drivers to go anywhere but straight back to the school after a game, but Mr. G. and that wonderful bus driver risked their livelihoods to stop at my house to bring the good news of our team's victory.

I saw that bus pull up while I was taking out the trash. Suddenly, my entire team piled out the bus door and onto my front lawn, yelling my name as they came. When I saw them, I almost burst into tears – I hadn't yet cried about my father, but it was so, so close. I ran inside and grabbed my family. Then we hauled food from our fridge – there was so much we'd been given! – and we went outside to greet everyone.

My teammates told all about the game and how we scored in the top of sixth inning to take the lead, and then we held off Monroe for the win.

Then they presented me with one of the greatest gifts I have ever received – the game ball.

The score of the game was written across the side of the baseball and every team member had signed it, including Mr. G. Again, I almost burst into tears.

Their actions that day changed me forever. I realized then that our family would get through this. With so many people caring for us and supporting us, there was no way this tragedy would defeat us. Suddenly, the odds were heavily stacked in our favor.

\* \* \*

Many of these heroic acts came from unexpected places, but there were some that came from people I already knew were heroes. One such person is my grandfather, Jack Kitson.

At the age of almost eighty, my grandpa has been through the Korean War, he's fought thousands of fires in the Bronx, and he and my grandmother raised a family of five kids. To this day, his brave and loving nature still inspires me.

Pop Pop has always been one of my most important role models, and after my father's death he continued to perform countless acts of selflessness to keep my family from falling apart. From visiting us every single morning for five years to accompanying my mother and me to the annual Troop 63 barbeque, he was always there for us. He never judged, he never became angry, and he never abandoned us. He simple stood by us silently and, once in a while, gently corrected any mistakes I made.

My grandpa has been my family's rock for six years on the day I am writing this. There is no one else like him, and I am so very proud to call him my grandfather.

*Grandma and Pop Pop*

As for Grandma – Grandma with the quick wit and even faster ability to show up when someone, especially my mom, needed her. The Kitson taxi would arrive with Pop Pop at the wheel and Grandma opening the door even before he came to a complete stop.

She was always there, hovering, hugging and basically doing – doing whatever needed to be done to make things a little easier for us. I'd open my eyes, and she'd be there walking dogs, cooking, cleaning, and asking – always asking how were we? Were we okay? Did we know she was there for us and always would be?

Grandma is the only person I know who laughs at herself quicker than anyone else does – her laughter brought out our smiles. At least I tried to smile. Trisha didn't and wouldn't – and honestly, she couldn't.

Grandma and Pop Pop even went on vacation with us eleven months after the funeral. There was Grandma, screaming and laughing on the The Mummy ride – screaming the entire way with her eyes closed but right there beside us. That's our Grandma – right there beside us, even if it means screaming the whole time. *Hello* is still her way of letting us know she is there for us always.

* * *

Another well established hero in our family is my Uncle Jimmy. A man who had also fought thousands of fires in New York City, saved countless lives, witnessed the attack on the World Trade Center, and won countless bar fights that he never started but always finished.

Without any kids of his own, he and my Aunt Diane adopted my sister and me. They made it their personal mission to protect us, guide us, and be there for us when our mother could not. It was Uncle Jimmy who stepped into the role of father when my own father left us.

He is infinitely wise and always knows what to do in any situation. Every day I strive to be as strong, smart, brave and funny as Uncle Jimmy. I do not have to tell him because I'm sure he already knows it, but I will say it anyway: Uncle Jimmy is one of the very few men on this earth who is a true hero.

* * *

Then there is the group of men who, you might say, have been my real-life avengers, if you will. Without them, I would never have attained my most challenging achievement. This group was known to us as the scoutmasters of Boy Scouts Troop 63. It was comprised of the fathers of my fellow scouts – Mr. Cassel, Mr. Albanese, Mr. Milosevic, Mr. Lisack, Mr. McLoughlin, and many more.

After my father's passing, these men took it upon themselves to make sure that I continued my Boy Scout career and eventually reach it highest rank. I am eternally grateful to them all, but there is one I would like to single out.

Mr. McLoughlin was the man who made my Eagle Scout project possible. He proposed the idea to me, helped form my plan, sat down with me every week to review my project write-up and prepared me for the final review.

He was there every step of the way for me. But his heroism went far beyond helping a young man complete his Eagle Scout project. If you have ever seen the film *The World Trade Center*, then you have seen Mr. McLoughlin. He is shown at the very end shaking hands with the actor who played him throughout the entire movie. That actor's name is Nicholas Cage.

Mr. McLoughlin, a Port Authority transit cop, was the last survivor to be rescued from the beneath the World Trade Center after the attacks of Sept. 11. He had been buried under the rubble for twenty-four hours before being rescued.

I am immeasurably grateful for what he has done, both for me and for this country.

\* \* \*

Probably my most consistent hero is my good friend Jared Lisack. Every single day for two years after my father's death, Jared was at my house, keeping me company and helping our family.

My mom referred to him as her second son.

Jared and I would walk to my house after school each day no matter the weather – sometimes walking through snow wearing our gym shorts. He showed me what friendship really is. The standard he set is one I aspire to.

How many heroes do you find in the skin of high school freshman?

\* \* \*

My sister Trisha is my hero on so many levels and in so many ways. She was only just twelve years old when Dad died – twelve! – and he was her hero, her best friend. Trisha and Daddy were starting to have almost the same walk just before he died.

*Twelve.*

Imagine that.

\* \* \*

My mother.

My mother is the strongest woman I have ever known. For six years, she has carried my sister and me across many miles and up many mountains. She is always, without fail, here for us.

Watching her during the first few years after my father's death was heartbreaking. She had the weight of raising two teenagers, supporting the household and keeping herself sane.

From my perspective, she did this remarkably well and – if I dare say it – with ease. At least that's how she made it seem to me. She seemed to have full confidence in herself, and that translated into my sister and I having full confidence in her. There was not a single moment when I doubted her.

Now she is finally moving on and has regained her happiness with her amazing husband, Gerard. And she has written this book, one that I hope can be a beacon of light for all women who find themselves thrust into such an incredibly tragic situation.

With my mom beside me, I feel anything is possible. Her life is proof of that. I love her fiercely.

Patricia Nelson, my mother, is the hero of this book and of my life. Thank you, Mom. You cannot imagine how much you mean to me.

\* \* \*

Finally, there is another sort of love. My last hero watched from afar as tragedy struck my family. Until we uncovered a photo of our old soccer team, we thought we hadn't met until our senior year in high school.

Her name is Jamie Rose Bradley, and she is the love of my life. The tattooed initials on my left wrist belong to her. They are there to remind me of the person who helped me rediscover happiness.

It began with a short, sweet kiss on the night of our homecoming dance. Jamie and I had been aware of each other, but we had never seen this coming. Although she was already taken by another, something inside drove me toward her. We began to text one another, and that was the sum of our relationship through much of our senior year.

But I wanted her. I stumbled forward in an effort to reel in the greatest catch of my life.

I started by somehow convincing this divine beauty that I needed help in math. Miraculously, she offered to tutor me. We met in the library for our first session. I already completely understood the chapter, but I sat next to her for hours pretending not to understand a word she was saying – and changing the subject every chance I got.

I claimed that her tutoring was making a world of difference, so we soon met again, this time at Panera's in Middletown. Again I pretended to be void of even the simplest of math skills. Again I tried to change the subject. Again we talked for hours.

Jamie told me that if I really needed help, I should find another tutor because we clearly could not focus on math.

*Jamie*

Eventually, I convinced her to tutor me at my house which, of course, turned into something other than tutoring. I know where your mind just ran, and you should be ashamed for thinking such a thing! Jamie is a classy broad, I tell you, and all we did was watch movies. The only move I made was to put my arm around her, I swear it. Cross my heart.

Anyway, the rest is history as they say. The prettiest girl I've ever seen became mine. With her came a prom date, a best friend and, I hope, a life-long love. Jamie Rose, you changed my life and saved my life. You are my very personal hero and you've made the last two years so very happy. I plan a lifetime of happiness for both of us.

* * *

The people on these pages have played an essential role in saving the Nelson family. I had no idea how much hope could come from losing all hope.

Heroes come from the most unlikely places and show up at the most unlikely times. But have faith that, when they are needed, they will show up.

All you have to do is open the door and let them in – and that can sometimes be the hard part.

# 23

## No Lectures – But a Bit of Advice

And now it is time for me to try to help others who find themselves in my shoes. If you're reading this book, it's possible you're already wearing them. We should talk.

Meanwhile, here are a few things I've learned these past five years:

Understand that your grief is as unique as you are. Once you recognize this, you will make peace with the fact that no one before you has gone through this in exactly the same way. A lot of people will offer a lot of good advice, but not all of it will apply to you, and not everyone will understand what you're feeling.

Yes, I learned some good and helpful things from the forty-plus books I read on grief, death, suicide, depression and widowhood. Yes, I was able to pick up a few tidbits from each book and incorporate these valuable items into my grief.

But there is no grief cookie cutter, so be prepared to do your grief like you have done your life – *your* way. You don't have a blueprint for how it's done, but you have you – your history, your personality, your style, your strengths, weaknesses, fears, hopes, biases, coping skills and safety net. You will need all of this to process your grief in the way it best suits you.

\* \* \*

Your relationships will change, some for the better, some for the worse. Death can bring out the worst in people, including those near and dear to you. The one you expect to be there the most might not be, and those who help the most might be people you never expected to see step up to the plate. Keep this in mind – those closest to you are also grieving, whether for you or because they, too, were close to the person who died.

On the other hand, not only did my husband shoot himself, but I lost friends because of this as well, and I still kind of resent that. Still, it's not worth holding a grudge toward someone who disappointed you in your time of need.

A very smart Life Coach told me, "You don't go to Macy's to buy milk," and it will become clear that there are certain people you don't go to for comfort. Learn who you can go to with what. If your best friend is suddenly busy every time you call, she may not be the person best suited to listen to you. If your mother-in-law tells you that "everyone has a cross to bear in life and this is yours, so you need to give thanks for all you have," she's not the one to go to, either – for much of anything.

\* \* \*

When you're having an especially bad day, try to identify why. When I do that – when I see that I'm in a funk because it would have been Howard's birthday tomorrow or it's the beginning of spring, I can chalk it up to that and not be hard on myself for backsliding for a day.

It's normal for me to be down at certain times and places. I went by the cemetery yesterday – not much happening there – but perhaps that hasn't helped my mood, either? In the past, I'd whine to someone or fill the empty spaces with cleaning or shopping or working out.

As time goes on, though, I try to take my own advice, identify the problem, and maybe just sit and BE for a while. These episodes occur less frequently now, but they do come back. Expect it, even five years down the road. Just let it happen. It's okay.

Of course, if your bad day extends to a bad couple of months, you might be suffering some clinical depression. Time to get professional help.

\* \* \*

Incorporate healthy activities and people and situations into your life. It may feel like a lot of work to get up and get moving or call people and make plans, but it actually, genuinely helps.

\* \* \*

Accept the fact that you will learn things about yourself that you may or may not like. Some things I've learned about myself:

I own way too many clothes

I waste way too much money

I've trusted some unsavory characters

I've run my body into the ground, even knowing it as I was doing it

I love conscious sedation when administered slowly like during a colonoscopy (I suppose there's something wrong in the fact I look forward to a colonoscopy because it means I get to sleep without stress or worry or dreams for at least one day following the procedure)

I still fear being alone

I'm not any good at meditating, but I'm working on it.

\* \* \*

It's a cliché, but in all honesty, time is the only thing that allows you to process what has happened to you. You cannot rush it or make things happen on your own time table. You don't even know what to process at first.

Meanwhile, accept whatever help is offered. Allow the love in. You need all the love and support you can get. And should you feel yourself too exposed under the microscope, just ask people to leave their reading glasses off so they don't see it all. A little privacy goes a long way.

\* \* \*

For those who are trying to help others work through their grief, here's a little advice for you as well:

Understand that there is no way a grieving widow and kids are capable of being as healthy as you are, even if you are also missing the person who died. Despite how upset or grieved you find yourself, trust me, they are much worse. That means you need to give the widow and kids the benefit of the doubt and not expect it to be the other way around.

Yes, we all have our crosses to bear but, believe it or not, some crosses are harder to bear than others. My kids losing their dad as young teenagers was a pretty big cross to bear. They needed all the love, support and assistance their families and friends could provide even if they weren't giving much back to the relationship. Cut them some slack.

\* \* \*

Trust me on this one – grieving people are never doing as well as you think they are. You might like to think otherwise, in part because that lets you off the hook a bit. But believe me when I tell you, they seem better than they are.

On the other hand, I confess I've gone to the other extreme and treated the kids as if they could not possibly be doing well at all. At times, I should have given them a little more credit. I had to learn not to assume anything and to really listen when they spoke. I also had to learn how to interpret the silence I sometimes got after I asked how they were.

\* \* \*

The most helpful, loving, kind and precious thing you can do for a grieving friend or relative is to just be present. Do something physical, even if it's just taking out the garbage. Listen if that is what the person needs.

Advice? Absolutely – give it, especially if it is from your heart, is relevant and kind. But do everyone a favor and, for God's sake, keep your judgments to yourself.

That's it. No more advice from me. It's your grief. You'll figure it out.

## 24

## Why Didn't I Know What I Knew?

There was a little voice deep, deep inside me telling me something bad was about to happen in the weeks before Howard killed himself. I know there must have been, but that message never found its way to my waking thoughts and consciousness.

Why did I know in my soul that something was terribly wrong, but I didn't know it in my head?

Was it God protecting me from the inevitable, protecting me from the full knowledge of something I couldn't prevent? Was He being kind by keeping me in the dark because, in the end, I couldn't change the course of events?

I think about it now, and it torments me.

Why did I wake from dreams speaking prayers but with no clear idea of why I was praying? Why was I plagued by a relentless, low-grade feeling that something terrible was going to happen?

My soul knew, but my consciousness didn't.

Looking back, I knew on some level that something was wrong two months before Howard killed himself, when I told him a friend might have committed suicide and his reaction was one of piqued interest, not sorrow or shock.

I knew on some level that something was wrong when I dragged Howard from therapist to therapist asking them to help him; asking for anything that would ease his pain, both physical and mental; asking Howard to *let* them help him.

I knew on some level that something was wrong on the Wednesday before Howard shot himself when I brought him to Good Samaritan Hospital with a severe headache. I *must* have known because I asked for a psych evaluation to determine if Howard was suicidal. Why did I do that? I don't know. He never threatened to kill himself. He denied he ever would when I asked.

But something deep inside compelled me to cry out for help, both in my sleep prayers and at the hospital. On that Friday, just before he was discharged at the start of that terrible Memorial Day weekend, I asked them to evaluate Howard once again for suicidal tendencies. They did, and they concluded he was not a risk. He loves you and the children far too much to kill himself, I was told.

I knew on some level that something was wrong when I brought him home from the hospital a changed man. The old Howard was back. Everyone noticed. But somewhere, deep in the recesses of my brain, I knew from nursing school that one of the major signs that someone is going to kill himself is that he suddenly becomes relaxed and happy.

Is that what drove me to keep checking on him throughout that Memorial Day weekend? Is that why I went to a barbecue at the Brinkley's next door only to jump the four-foot fence every fifteen minutes to check on him as he lay in bed?

My heart races now as I relive those days. Why didn't I know what my soul knew, what I must have known on my body's cellular level? What was blocking it from arriving at my conscious mind? Perhaps it was simply that I refused to acknowledge it? I hope it wasn't that.

On one hand, I was trying to keep an eye on Howard, to keep him from – yes – from hurting himself. So why didn't I remove the guns from the house? Why didn't I know what I knew?

The Goshen Village Police have Howard's suicide note. I've seen it; the kids have not, which is why it doesn't appear here. Besides, the note didn't adequately answer the "Why?" question.

He was sorry, he said; he loved us, he said; don't do a big deal funeral, he said.

As suicide notes go, it was kind of boring, but perhaps they all are. After all the suffering and change Howard's suicide wrought, his last words were almost kind of anti-climactic – almost a fill-in-the-blanks suicide note that could have been written by anyone.

More than anything, that note reveals only that he was already gone when he wrote it. All that was left for him was to pull the trigger.

Like I told Diesel when he was barking at the thunder, we're never going to figure it out. Not completely.

But as I discovered, figuring it out doesn't mean we can't move on. A few unanswered questions shouldn't stand in the way of hope.

Sometimes, we just have to let it go at that.

## Luke's Toast

### April 06, 2013

As best man for his new stepfather when Trish and Gerard married, it fell to Luke Nelson to give the wedding toast.

It is both ironic and fitting that the last thing Luke did for his father on the day he died was to make him toast, and the first thing he did for his stepfather on his wedding day, nearly six years later, was to make an altogether different kind of toast.

Both were acts of such generosity, kindness and love.

Here is Luke's wedding toast.

## One Favor

I will start from the beginning
As a soul rises to heaven, angels singing

A woman and her children are left behind
But they'll be damned if their lives will be resigned

A struggle ensues for many years
Filled with hardships and many tears

The woman waits for a husband and her children a dad
  The empty void leaves them alone, broken and sad

  Men try to fill the hole that's grown so deep
Though for most the hill they must climb proves too steep

  There was one, however, who did reach the top
He's German, after all, I hear they mountain climb a lot

  In swooped our hero, ready to fight
  To help our devastated family reunite

  Imagine the joy when he actually succeeded
And the family's painful past would no longer be repeated

  They became whole again, on a sunny day in spring
Before family and friends, the woman received her ring

  Our knight and his five canine squires
Make a perfect fit for what this family requires

  This tragic tale full of twists and bends
   Will finally rest at a happy end

My mom now has a husband, my sister and I a father
  By the world, we will no longer be bothered

Now I must ask one favor of all in this room
Please help my new family start off with a boom!

Luke Nelson

*The wedding toast*

# Epilogue

## May 2013

    Trish and her kids and dogs are gone from Oxford Road now.

    She and Gerard Schaffner were married on April 6, 2013, nearly six years after Howard's suicide. Gerard won the approval of Trish's family, friends and the neighbors immediately and unanimously. The wedding was the most joyous celebration in anyone's memory.

    Trisha and Luke were the couple's honor attendants. Astro, Gerard's little Maltese, served as ring bearer, thereby representing the couple's combined seven dogs at the ceremony. He sat quietly through the wedding, then sounded out a few happy barks at just the right moment – when the couple's guests began clapping and cheering at the end of the vows.

    Trish and Gerard live in northern New Jersey, at least for now. His dog training, grooming and day care business is there, and it's less than an hour's ride to Trish's job and her extended family of relatives and friends. It's too far, though, for Jack to bring the dogs their buttered rolls each morning.

Luke and Trisha are in college, starting to live the chapters of their own adult lives. They are a triumph of reason, sweetness, humor and dignity.

Diesel and Daisy – well, Diesel's heart is still a little broken. He never really got over Howard's disappearance from his life. Daisy still gets skittish at the sound of loud, sudden noises. But all in all, they're happy to be part of an expanded canine family. They spend their days now playing with the guests at Gerard's dog day care center. It is a good life.

The people of Oxford Road have gone on with their own lives. Scott and Danielle moved to Chattanooga, Tennessee, a couple of years ago where Scott got a terrific job despite an uncertain job market. Craig and Sara have two little girls now. Mark and Meri still listen to the top 100 countdown on Memorial Day. The Mills, the Quinns, Joe Bayno – they're all still there.

Everyone on the street has been slow to get to know the new neighbors who now live in the Nelson house. It is still Trish's house, as far as they're concerned. It's hard to think of it otherwise.

Still, Howard's suicide changed the street for the better in some ways. That summer, almost as though they were following Diesel and Daisy's lead, the neighbors began to spend more time out front instead of in the privacy of their back yards.

"We have that big back deck, but we're more likely to sit on the front porch steps in the evening now," said Craig Benson.

Some nights during the warm weather, there are impromptu parties on the street. "Trailer trash parties," everyone calls them. It's usually Heather and Carl Morse at No. 13 who get things rolling when they haul their fire pit out to the end of their driveway. Then the neighbors begin drifting toward the fire with a bottle of beer or wine and a folding chair.

"It's not a street anymore," said Harry Mills. "It's a neighborhood now."

* * *

Those who knew Howard Nelson still struggle to understand how he could have left Luke and Trisha, Diesel and Daisy and Trish behind. There remains a mix of anger and sadness in their hearts.

"I was mad at Howie for a year," said Steve O'Sullivan, Howard's closest friend at the firehouse. "I loved him like a brother. We both worked nights and did our drills together during the day. We called ourselves the You and Me Team.

"And then he left. He was gone, and I was just the Me Team."

That mix of love and hurt and anger was perhaps best summed up by Trish's brother-in-law Richie when his daughter Rachel asked him what he'll do when he sees Howard in heaven.

"Well, first I'm going to punch him," Richie told his daughter. "Then ... well, then I'm going to reach out my hand and help him up off the floor. And then I'm going to give him a big bear hug and tell him how much I love him."

*Howard John Nelson*

*March 29, 1955*

*May 30, 2007*

# Acknowledgments

I will forever be grateful to the countless people who have not only walked this journey with me, but who have made my life the beautiful bounty it is today.

It was my chance encounter with Beth Quinn during a walk through the streets of Goshen that first inspired me to make a book out of the endless pages I had written since Howard's death. As my neighbor, friend and editor, Beth's belief in the words on these pages is the reason there is a book. She has my sincere gratitude for her talent and time.

I am forever grateful for the people in my life who *are* my life: My parents John and Mary Kitson, who remain our family's steadfast supporters with endless love and their total beings; my siblings Johnny, Jimmy, Kathy and Ann, with whom I share an unbreakable bond (and some really funny stories); my amazing and loving in-laws Nora, Diane, Richie and Russ, who have allowed the Kitson clan to surround them (and often dominate the conversations); my nieces and nephews, the Cousins Club (aka the *Hennelshakkits* Club), who have shown their great love for their cousins Trisha and Luke by allowing them to just be who they are.

I am indebted to my neighbors on Oxford Road, whose endless support, front lawn parties and laughter helped the kids and me through the roughest of times. You will always be my neighbors and great friends no matter where we may live.

Thank you to the various friends, acquaintances, parents, firemen, school personnel and walking partners I ran into on my daily rounds in Goshen. Thanks for your smiles, prayers and acts of kindness. It *does t*ake a village and Goshen took care of us.

My childhood girlfriends and I remain each other's staunchest supporters. I never laugh louder or harder than when I am with Margy, Peggy, Patty, Murph, Sheryl, Kelly and the others. Our trips, girls nights, and hanging-out time together helped me get back to who I used to be before tragedy consumed me. I look forward to our next fifty years together, and I still plan on building that Childhood Girlfriends Senior Home in The Villages for us all.

Diesel and Daisy, too, have my gratitude. Our countless hours together on walks, our hugs, our mutual need to love and be loved helped keep my mind focused on moving forward – even if it was just putting one paw in front of the others as we traipsed the village streets together.

My Gerard – well, here came happiness barreling into my life just when I was getting comfortable being a single girl. His confidence in this project convinced me to remain committed. Without him, this book would not have been finished. I love you, Gerard.

And, of course, my Luke and my Trisha have all of my love and gratitude. After all, they were the only reason I got up in the morning for a long, long time. This is for you.

If you or someone you know needs help ...
please call.

### National Suicide Hotlines
1-800-SUICIDE/1-800-784-2433

1-800-273-TALK/1-800-273-8255

1-877-YOUTHLINE/1-877-968-8454

1-877-VET-2-VET/1-877-838-2838

1-800-799-4TTY/1-800-799-4889 (hearing impaired)

### Local Suicide Hotlines
Dutchess County: 845-485-9700

Orange County: 1-800-832-1200

Ulster County: 845-255-8801/845-679-2485

OR

Call 911 and ask for help.

Tell the operator you are in suicidal danger.

To order additional copies of this book, please visit itwasnoaccident.com.

Made in the USA
Charleston, SC
06 October 2013